Organizational Engineering

Organizational Engineering

✦

Management is Out! Engineering is In!

Paul Kartinen

iUniverse, Inc.

New York Lincoln Shanghai

Organizational Engineering
Management is Out! Engineering is In!

iUniverse, Inc.

For information address:
iUniverse, Inc.
2021 Pine Lake Road, Suite 100
Lincoln, NE 68512
www.iuniverse.com

ISBN: 0-595-30676-4

Contents

Thanks For The Journey
(Acknowledgements)

The journey to *Organizational Engineering* took almost forty years. It began in the former Bethlehem Steel Corporation Shipbuilding Division shipyard in the Los Angeles harbor. Shortly after receiving a B.S. in Engineering and a transfer to the San Francisco yard, I was selected as the single participant in an experimental management development program. Experience in every facet of the yard's operation was combined with exposure to a variety of ivory-tower academics in organizational management. Mixing real life industrial situations with academic theory turned out to be much more productive than receiving another academic diploma to hang on the wall, an option not chosen. I thank the (former) Bethlehem Steel Corporation and in particular Mr. Pat Filip, then General Manager of the San Francisco Yard, for their considerable two-year investment.

Shortly after completion of the program I relocated to the Los Angeles harbor yard, then was directed to rebuild an ailing department. I thank Mr. A. J. Maloney, General Manager at the time, for the opportunity at such an early stage in my career to apply and develop those newly generated organizational skills.

Additional assignments at both of those west coast yards consumed the rest of my seventeen-year tenure with the Bethlehem Steel Corporation. (The corporation decided to considerably reduce their shipyard operations in the early 1980s.) The variety of activities and responsibilities Bethlehem afforded me laid the groundwork for *Organizational Engineering*.

The closure of the shipyards plunged me into a brief interlude, during the recession of the early 1980s, before my next long-term employment with a major corporation. I thank Pacific Cartage and Warehousing in Hayward, California for the opportunity to again test the organizational concept I had developed from the shipyard experiences. That short exercise as Vice President of Warehouse Operations confirmed the concept. I also thank the Royal Saudi Naval Force for an interesting term as head of the Maintenance Management Division for the RSNF. That exposure provided unique situations to test the theories of *Organizational Engineering*.

The journey to *Organizational Engineering* concluded with a sixteen year "education" with The Boeing Company at the Fabrication Division of The Boeing Commercial Airplane Group. I wish to thank the several crew leaders at the Auburn, Washington plant for the opportunity to act as a consultant in structuring, changing, and operating their departments. I also wish to thank the multiple corporate executives who resided near the top of a rather monstrous organization chart. Their actions well demonstrated the ill-effects that inappropriate management techniques cast upon an organization's internal workings. The experience persuaded me to attempt something new and exciting: documenting this concept of organizational engineering.

Paul

Introduction

Engineers design and construct structures and machines. They deal in basically two things: (1) materials, and (2) the scientific principles that dictate how those materials will behave when put to use. Several years of study are required to understand materials and the science that guides putting them to use.

Most of us have heard of mechanical, electrical, and structural engineers. They specialize in certain materials and in certain scientific principles peculiar to their field. Relatively few of us have heard of "Organizational Engineers." But, we probably recognize the word "Management" as referring to the job of operating organizations. Unfortunately, my experience at large corporations has shown that management has evolved into a very complex, confusing subject. It seems to have lost its original meaning and has become so complex that most "managers" don't even know what management is anymore. So it has come to this: organizational engineers, not managers, design and construct organizations. And like other engineers, organizational engineers deal with a very specific material that behaves according to scientific principles.

There is a seemingly infinite supply of concepts, theories, philosophies, and just plain outrageous opinions on how to get human beings together to get something done. Some of these ideas claim there are different methods to be used on big versus little projects, for big versus little organizations. And, a lot of excuses are made for big organizations that are very inefficient. Those excuses are unacceptable. Are they inefficient because they're big, or are they big because they're inefficient?

Along with that infinite supply of ideas has also come an infinite supply of people, pumped out of business schools with advanced degrees. (Some become "instant experts," consultants who have never managed an organization.) I've studied with some, worked with some, and watched some. Unfortunately, something seems to be missing in all these managers; it seems there are very few who actually understand how to apply an effective management technique, how to run an organization the way it should be run, using all the skills of all the people, not just a select few.

And then there are those skilled electricians, mechanics, doctors, and engineers who have been thrown into management positions without any business or management training at all. Their new job can be quite baffling to them. It is one thing to be an automotive mechanic, quite another to manage an auto repair shop. One supervisor at a large company told me: " On Friday I used a wrench. On Monday I was a manager. I didn't know what to do, and after three years still don't."

All of these people need help. The mad dashes from one management concept to another, then to the next "philosophy of the month" only end in failure. These people need to become organizational engineers. Large organization or small, Organizational Engineering is the key to success. It replaces management with a simple, understandable, successful process.

Decades ago I was given the opportunity to study something called "professional management." The simplest definition of management I heard back then was: "Getting things done through other people." I'm sure that fancier words are now used to define it, but the impressive thing about this simple definition is that it has all the elements that are relevant to organizations. There are things to do, some action to take, and people involved.

Unfortunately, there is hazardous ground here. Failure results from misinterpretation of one small, apparently innocent phrase: "…through other people." You wouldn't think this little phrase could be a problem, but it is. It is a huge problem. This simple phrase can imply that, as a manager, you don't have to know anything or do much of anything because other people are doing the work to get the thing done. My experience has shown this to be a reality. Many people in management don't seem to know what they are to do when they walk into work each day.

If we hire an electrician to do electrical work for our factory, we make sure our new employee knows electrical theory, circuitry and hardware; they've been trained to do what they do. And, if they don't do it well we've got to make a change, fast. Electrical fires and dead circuits are not acceptable. However, that doesn't seem to be the case with management people. There are lots of people in management positions who haven't a clue about what management work is, or how to do it. They simply don't know how to manage. It's not necessarily their fault; someone may have put them in that position. Unfortunately, while the inept electrician is out the incompetent manager stays and quite often is promoted to an even more crucial position.

So, it would seem prudent to change the simple definition of management to: "Getting things done through people, including the boss." "Other" is out; "the boss" is in. This means that even the boss, the manager, has something to do to help get things done. And, like electricians, managers must have some skills to do their part. They must be trained in how to set up and operate the organization. Yes, ~~management~~ Organizational Engineering is a learned skill with certain rules of the road and things to be done to get all the other people together to do the thing. The electrician must know electrical stuff; the ~~manager~~ organizational engineer must know Organizational Engineering. These few pages will show these managers what they need to do when they walk into work each day. They will become organizational engineers. "Management" is out; "Organizational Engineering" is in.

Organizational Engineering is something to be learned, just like other fields of engineering. In fact, experience has shown me that it is very similar to the other fields of engineering. Scientific principles of very special materials—people—are applied to a logical process to form those materials into a useful machine, an organization. **Organizational Engineering is the profession of designing and operating a group of people, an organization, to do something**; it is "getting things done through people, including the boss." Mechanical engineers design and construct machines to get something done. Organizational engineers design and operate groups of people to get something done.

It may sound inhumane to refer to people as materials, especially materials that can be manipulated by using a few scientific principles. Well, that is not the case at all. Some people believe that the typical worker is lazy, stupid, doesn't want to work. Some people operate organizations in which it appears the workers are lazy and don't want to work. I have found there are not millions of lazy, stupid workers; there are millions of workers trapped in "mismanaged" organizations, their talents and energy wasted by lousy management. This is very frustrating because it does not have to be this way, and it is easy to solve. In these few pages you will see that Organizational Engineering is actually a tribute to the amazing skills people possess and to their innate, positive drive to perform and succeed. People are the most valuable "materials" under the sun. They can do amazing things, given the chance.

As a matter of fact, this whole thing reminds me of the sun. Standing in the sun, you can feel its power, even from more than ninety million miles away. Think of all the potential energy in the sun. I have found that a group of people has that same energy. Unfortunately, very few organizations actually capture and use that energy; it is wasted. Poorly managed, these organizations realize only an infinitesimal portion of all the potential energy in a group of people. This discussion of Organizational Engineering will describe how to unleash all that power.

This book is very short, very simple. How can the subject of management be covered so briefly? There are billions of words on millions of pages all dedicated to the subject. That's the problem; management has become a confusing, complicated subject. It has become a mess. Yes, there are a lot of details in designing and operating an organization, but the actual process of setting up and watching your organization is quite simple, so simple that no one seems to do it. They're too busy managing and don't seem to have the time or skills to get organized. Thus, "managed organizations" end up to be big, complicated messes instead of simple, efficiently engineered businesses and operations.

What you are about to read is nothing more than common sense, the obvious. As you read you'll be thinking: "I know that." This is to be a simple discussion about being successful. It will put all of those "I-know-that"s together into a logical method to organize and operate either a single project or an on-going organization. And, this logical method can be applied to any organization that has a job to do.

In the early 1970's I was the only participant in a corporation's experimental management development program. Since then I have spent decades studying, establishing, operating and changing organizations. Experience with people from all walks of life in all kinds of endeavors has resulted in the few pages that follow. The scientific principles and organizational process described have been found to be a practical, understandable simplification of the complexity that organizational management has become. So, whether you're building a deck in your backyard, operating a charity, running a public school system, or joined with 100,000 people making rocket ships, these few pages are your guide to getting your thing done, and done efficiently. At the same time everyone involved in your organization will grow and prosper.

Paul

Organizations

Why do companies, corporations, charities, any organizations exist? The answer is quite obvious when you think about it. Consider our definition of Organizational Engineering: "Getting things done through people, including the boss." Organizations exist to get something done. That's it. Seems pretty simple, obvious, maybe not even worth discussing. But, you'd be surprised how many organizations become confused just because somewhere along the way people forget why their organization exists. Sound unreal? It happens.

Some years ago I was involved with one of those mega-corporations with lots of departments manufacturing products. Considerable effort had been made by a manufacturing department to design a more efficient way to operate the factory. It involved a few changes in what various people would do and how they would interact with each other. Everyone on the manufacturing floor was excited and ready to go. Then, disaster struck. Some big shots in the human relations/personnel department at the corporate office became aware of the activities. Management folks from the factory were called to the corporate office. They took with them one worker bee who had been deeply involved in formulating the new operating methods with all of the people doing the work on the production floor. Since he understood the details of the changes, the worker bee described the activities leading up to the decision to change things, what the changes were, and how the changes would improve production. Everyone on the manufacturing floor was ready to roll because it was obvious that a very inefficient, confusing workplace was going to become smarter, more efficient. This would result in higher productivity and a more rewarding work-life for the floor personnel.

Well, the corporate suits shut it down! The big guns in a support department (human relations/personnel) were afraid the union would file grievances. And for some reason, the suits had the power to tell the people in the manufacturing departments how to run their business—a major, major management error. People twenty miles away, who never set foot on the factory floor, were allowed to tell the factory floor people they couldn't do it. And, the people who wanted to make the changes were union members themselves. Disaster.

This is a perfect example of people forgetting why an organization exists in the first place. The company was in the business of manufacturing a product; that was the reason for its existence. But, the suits in personnel had forgotten that. Apparently they thought the factory was set up to employ people who wouldn't file grievances, not to make products. To this day that company is still a frustrating, inefficient organization. (It's amazing that it still exists. But that's another story.)

This should not happen. The very reason for an organization to exist should not be attacked. As in our example, when the reason for an organization's existence is pushed aside the organization and the people involved suffer. An easy life for the personnel department took the place of producing the product. The company's bottom line suffered. The people on the manufacturing floor became even more frustrated and angrier; they had been sentenced to an unfulfilling, marginally productive work-life. It is extremely important to remember and demand that everyone shoot at the same target, that target being the reason the organization exists, the thing it was created to do.

So, we've struck a basic chord here. Organizations exist to get something done. They are not created to hire people, sweep the floor or worry about grievances.

The fact that organizations are first and foremost created to do something, fulfill a need or chase an exciting possibility, can at times lead to some very unpleasant circumstances. Sometimes things change; maybe no one needs your product or services anymore. People may be laid off or moved to other, less comfortable positions requiring new skills. Anything can happen depending upon the thing the organization must do. But, "the thing", which we will call The Task of the organization, is the reason for existence. All else revolves around getting it done.

But how does this all fit in with those grand words about people having the power of the sun and being the most valuable material on earth? How can we push people around just because the organization's "thing" changes or maybe even disappears altogether? The scientific principles and the organizational engineering design process will show you how it all comes together. It will become obvious that focusing on The Task of the organization is the best thing for both the organization and for the people involved.

Organizations exist to do something. The Task comes first.

Yes, **The Task comes first**. Organizational design is based upon this fact. The Task is the beginning of all organizational life. It is the starting point of the Organizational Engineering process. Yes, **designing and operating an organization is a process. The organizational engineer orchestrates a process to construct and operate an organization to do The Task.** And, because the basic material is people, the engineer must know the scientific principles to effectively tap into the amazing energy and power of people.

Therefore, **Organizational Engineering consists of two distinct yet very related subjects: (1) the scientific principles** which unleash the energy of that most valuable of materials, people, and **(2) the organizational design and operating process** which is the logical method to construct, operate, watch and change the organization. The scientific principles are to be consistently used throughout the design and operating process. They are key to achieving success in both the initial design as well as the continued operation of the organization. So, we will address those scientific principles first.

The Scientific Principles of
Organizational Engineering

Engineers who design machinery contend with the science of Mother Nature. There are a myriad of physical and chemical principles to know about the materials used to make something. Organizational engineers are somewhat luckier. It is ironic that even though they deal with one of the most complicated materials, people, while designing and operating organizations, organizational engineers must contend with very few Scientific Principles. In fact, there are only four. Yes, the organizational engineer really needs to know and apply only four basic Principles while he/she executes the organizational design and operating process.

Organizational Engineering is a simple process, very simple. The four Scientific Principles are also simple. Sometimes this simplicity presents a problem. The Principles are so simple, so obvious some people are skeptical that just these four basic concepts are all that the engineers need to remember and apply when designing and operating an organization. They either complicate them by reading more into them than they should, or they neglect them because such simplicity cannot possibly be the answer to all the complex problems people can present. People present problems only when they are trapped in a poorly managed organization, one that does not apply the four Principles. As unbelievable as it may sound, use of these four Principles just about eliminates people problems.

So, do not neglect these Principles in your rush to organize. Problems await the organization that does not use them. If a structural engineer designs something to sit in the ocean but forgets the chemical principle that seawater corrodes mild steel bolts, the thing will rust away and fall apart. Neglecting an organizational engineering Principle will also result in a "rusted, busted" organization. The organizational engineer must fully understand and apply the Scientific Principles during the entire organizational engineering process.

Principle #1—To successfully get something done that requires a group to do, the whole group must want to get the same thing done. Seems rather obvious, a really simple thing to understand and apply, makes sense. If you want a deck on the back of your house you shouldn't hire Fred if he insists on building you a doghouse. This is not rocket science, but, unfortunately, this principle can be an elusive creature to actually apply, apply all the time.

One would think that this concept is so obvious that Principle #1 is not even worth considering when mired in the mess and confusion of organizing to do The Task. That's the very point—stay out of the mess and confusion when performing the organizational engineering process. Organizational Engineering is simple, no mess or confusion. Remember our story about the mega-corporation? A personnel department was allowed to crush some important improvements on the manufacturing floor. Why, because not everyone wanted to do the same thing. Principle #1 was broken, forgotten, neglected. The factory floor existed to make the company's product, doing the thing the company was formed to do. But, the personnel department had something else in mind. Not everyone wanted to do the same thing when they walked into work each day. The factory floor, the people, the company, even the consumer who pays the bill for the inefficiency all suffered.

Principle #2—The best place to control something is where that something takes place. Again, it's obvious. The best place to steer the car is behind the steering wheel. When the light turns green the person at the steering wheel who pushes the gas pedal is in the best place, the only place, to get the car moving in the right direction.

That same factory floor incident comes to mind again. The people on the floor who did the work, who wanted to improve the production methods were going to increase their productivity. But, for some reason people twenty miles away who never even saw the factory floor were allowed to shut them down. Principle #2 was absolutely trashed. Even though they didn't know it, those "in control" were allowed to trash their own organization. They were twenty miles away, not able to understand the production floor operations. It was a disaster.

On the other hand, I have seen this Principle in action. An entire process was vastly improved because someone used it, fully. There were two separate departments in an industrial plant: a transportation department and a maintenance department. The transportation department was responsible for moving materials and people throughout the plant. The maintenance crew kept the transportation equipment in good running order. Both the transportation system and maintenance procedures were transformed by initiating a new "vision" of the work these groups did. Drivers and mechanics joined forces and shifted gears (so to speak) from driving and maintaining to "supplying transportation needs of the plant," an expanded job for those people. Their thing to do, the Task, was transformed from changing spark plugs and steering a forklift to providing a major function, a process, for the plant. After all, the reason for having them around was to provide transportation. The people directly involved in the (transportation) process were allowed to control their work, control their responsibility, control their job. They joined forces to select and operate equipment to suit the need. Transportation service got better and maintenance costs were significantly reduced.

Why did transportation get better? What happens when you allow the experts on the subject to control their business? Who is better qualified to know about operating equipment than those who do it? Who is better at judging how well equipment will hold up than those who maintain and fix it? It's quite obvious; let the experts control their job.

But, care must be taken in applying this Principle. Principle 2 has been misapplied by something that has become quite popular— "pushing decisions down" (the organization chart). Principle #2 says things should be done, decided where they happen. Pushing decisions down is not always the intelligent thing to do. This Principle requires that decision-making is done in the right place, where the subject at hand happens. Some managers try pushing down decisions that they should make. Remember, the organizational engineer is responsible for the final look and operation of the organization. He is the conductor of the orchestra who knows that the violin must play these notes while the flute plays those notes. Yes, the engineer deeply involves the people performing the process, but the final creation of the organization's structure and operation is the engineer's job. The worker performs the work; the organizational engineer designs and operates the organization.

Principle #3—The more information people are given about things that affect getting results, the more they will work to reach those results. ("If you think training is expensive, try ignorance.") This is a huge, important concept—communication. This principle is the key to developing informed, thinking, and motivated people. Successful organizations depend upon the knowledge of their people.

There is a phrase used all too often which is the antithesis of this Principle. Disasters are built from the use of these few seemingly innocent words: "…need to know basis." This phrase means that someone decides not to tell people things. Time and again this "non-communication" concept is used to hide, protect, shield important information from the very people who should know things. People in an organization should know things, everything. They cannot help the organization succeed if they do not know all about its Task, the conditions under which it is operating (e.g. government regulations, finances, competition, etc.), how their efforts integrate with others in the organization, and on and on. People should know everything.

Years ago I started using a method that may help force communication to become a habit. "Never Say No" forces communication. Let's say someone in your organization has an idea to improve or change a procedure, but your immediate reaction is to say "No, that won't work." Well, you can't say that; this technique doesn't allow it. It requires you to discuss the reason that you want to say no. (By the way, if you don't have a reason for wanting to say no you've got another problem we won't address here.) What is the possible outcome of this discussion? Either your feelings are right and have a sound basis for not agreeing with the idea, or you are wrong and require some new information yourself. What happens? Either you impart new information to that person or they impart new information to you. This is a win-win concept. Somebody learns something; usually both people learn something. And, there are a lot of side benefits like developing trust and confidence in each other, an important part of strengthening your organization of people. This may take a lot of time at first, trying to teach each other everything. But, it is well worth the effort. Everyone becomes an active, productive part of the organization.

And, there is no such thing as information overload. Yes, there may be too much information, but informed people who are pointed at a target (Principle 1) can assimilate, judge and retain what they need. The transportation people in the above discussion needed to know a lot of stuff, stuff other than operating a forklift or changing spark plugs. It took months to help them understand business, accounting, the plant's transportation needs, etc. It took months to bring them up to speed so they could operate their own business. They took on the job and did it better than anyone else could. The experts controlled their own process through knowledge, which resulted from lots of communication. They helped decide how to provide transportation. (A perfect lead-in to the last Principle.)

Principle #4—People given the chance to help decide how to get something done will then want to get it done. Time and again I have seen people sit in a corner, decide how something shall happen, they think, and then toss it out to the rest of the organization as the new procedure or policy. It is never accepted. First, many heads, especially knowledgeable heads, are better than one. Second, people do not like getting something crammed down their throats, especially things that are flawed, confused, and complex.

On the other hand, people will work very hard to make their ideas become successful. Motivation and empowerment are terms used to describe the results of using this Principle. However, there are things to recognize when using this Principle. Read Principle 4 closely. I have seen managers try this idea with no success or outright disaster as the result. They toss out The Task then have everyone else formulate how to get it done without being personally involved. (I call this MBI—management by isolation.) Big mistake; this does not work. Principle 4 says that everyone must "help"; it is still up to the organizational engineer to design and operate the organization. Why do you think the football coach is on the playing field during the game? He is needed; he is the leader of the pack. A smart coach absorbs information from the entire team, but it is the coach's job to decide the strategy of the game. Organizational engineers are part of the game. They must not be isolated. They can neither exercise the Principles nor do their job if they are not where the action is. They cannot control their job, Principle 2.

So, the organizational engineer works with everyone involved to develop methods and procedures to accomplish The Task. However, and this is vitally important, **the final structure and operating processes of the organization are the responsibility of the organizational engineer.** Communication (Principle 3) and this participation by everyone are the key to motivating the entire group. Motivation, motivation, motivation—the sun's power unleashed. Using this Principle, combined with Principle 3, goes a long, long way to achieving an efficient organization.

Reread the Principles.

Principle #1—To successfully get something done that requires a group to do, the whole group must want to get the same thing done.

Principle #2—The best place to control something is where that something takes place.

Principle #3—The more information people are given about things that affect getting results, the more they will work to reach those results.

Principle #4—People given the chance to help decide how to get something done will then want to get it done.

Perhaps you have perceived by now that The Principles are intertwined; they all are involved with each other. Imagine a house with just walls, or just a roof, or just a floor. You need all the pieces to make a house do what it is suppose to do. The Principles are all used to design and operate the organization. Your organization will not gain that power of the sun in people without understanding and applying all four Principles, all the time.

Take our transportation example. Everyone involved had to want to help the plant operate smoothly and efficiently in doing what it did. They all had to "…want to get the same thing done." (Principle 1) They recognized the importance of transportation to the plant's operation and wanted to do the best they could. Then, and only then, could the organizational engineer allow them to control their job (Principle 2) by providing them with information (Principle 3) and allowing them to help formulate the structure and operating processes of the transportation department (Principle 4).

Our example of the personnel department shutting down an improvement on a factory floor is a perfect, real-life experience in the destruction of Principle 2. From twenty miles away the personnel department "controlled", or thought they controlled, what happened on the factory floor. Although unrecognized by the big shots, the company suffered a major setback. Principles 1, 3 and 4 had been used to gain the production workers' interest in the company by allowing them to volunteer valuable inputs to improve their factory and elevate their performance to higher level. But, ignoring just that one Principle (2) really destroyed the factory floor environment. The company suffered, suffered more than the big shots would ever know. Just as the structural engineer should recognize that seawater corrodes a mild steel bolt, the organizational engineer should recognize that neglecting the Scientific Principles just as surely corrodes the organization.

The Organizational Design and Operating Process

In my college days of the 1960s I worked in a ship repair yard during summer breaks. Ship repair yards are kind of like repair garages for cars except they work on ships; they fix ships not cars. I worked in the maintenance crew that took care of the yard and equipment used to repair ships. Not being stuck in one place doing the same thing all day, I could roam around the entire yard, seeing and working on everything. I could see everything that was going on, even in the offices.

I started to notice what people were doing in the shipyard. There were people who actually did the work of repairing the ships for the customers. They were not all on the ships, turning wrenches or welding steel. There were people in offices and buildings, not on ships; they did things that directly helped get the ship work done. They would buy materials, stock/issue nuts and bolts and other things in a warehouse, do accounting work to track and report the costs of doing the work, even finish the job by documenting the work done and getting the owner of the ship to pay the bill. All these people were doing things that had to happen to do what the shipyard was built to do: get customers; fix their ships; get them to pay the bill. Some of the people were in offices; some were on the ships. It was quite a busy place when you stopped to watch it all.

It took a bit longer to notice the second group of people. These folks didn't actually work on the ships themselves, buy parts from vendors, do the accounting work, or talk the customer into paying the bill. They stood around and watched; they talked to people. There weren't nearly as many of them as those doing the ship work. Then, I saw an organization chart. It turned out that these people were "over-seeing" the different functions happening to get all the ship work done. The top box on the chart was called "General Manager." These folks were managers.

The whole thing turns out to be rather simple. There are two kinds of work. Let's call them "productive work" and "Organizational Engineering work", formerly called management. The productive work consists of those things being done by people who do "The Task" of the organization, the thing to get done. They do what the organization was actually set up to do. Some people now call this work "value added." It fulfills the desires of the customer; it does what the organization has been established to do. All other activity, including Organizational Engineering, is called "non-value added" work, which doesn't directly fix the ship. But, Organizational Engineering is actually quite valuable; it needs to be done. On the other hand, it does not directly do The Task of the organization. So, productive work should be efficiently maximized while Organizational Engineering should be kept to a minimum. Organizational Engineering should be simple, yet complete. That's where "management" has failed; it has become too complex.

Organizational Engineering is a process used to get something done efficiently. It sets up and operates an organization to do its thing, its Task. Success relies on a couple of basic phenomena. First, people can be smarter than we usually give them a chance to be. They can do more for the organization than we let them do. And, they are the key ingredients to success. The Scientific Principles are the key to realizing that power of the sun. Second, almost any organizational structure you set up will work as long as it is a "process organization" structure, and you execute it using the Organizational Design and Operating Process (summarized in this chapter and detailed in subsequent chapters) to set up and operate that structure. Yes, that's what Organizational Engineering is all about: Process Organizations, how to design and operate them by allowing people to use their intelligence, knowledge, and skills.

Let's make this clear. Organizational Engineering is not a production process, like how to fix a pump on a ship. It is how to set up and operate an organization of people to get something done. These are entirely different concepts; organizational engineers have entirely different jobs than production people.

Many organizations fall into a trap. They set up organizations by bunching people with certain skills together and then say: "Okay, now how do we get these people to do what we want them to do?" Or, worse yet: "Now, what shall we have these people do?" As crazy as this sounds, I've seen it happen. It's absolutely flabbergasting. Skill-oriented, lumps-of-people organizations find it very difficult to do their thing. People work in turmoil. Not much gets done. The management is constantly reorganizing, trying to find the magic solution to the problems they've caused. This type of organization does not work because it does not recognize the reason for its existence. It's thinking about lumps of people instead of The Task, the very foundation of organizational life.

Any complex subject is merely a series of simple steps. Getting an organization together to accomplish something is complex. But by breaking down the job of organizing into a series of simple steps, you will find getting people together to do something won't seem so difficult. This organizational engineering process consists of fifteen steps; the steps create and operate a process organization. The first eleven steps are "What To Do." They identify The Task and establish a plan of how to accomplish it. Steps 12 and 13, "Doing It," are exciting; they unleash all that power of the sun in people. The organizational engineer then watches the action in steps 14 and 15 to detect any operating problems while also remaining open for any changes in The Task, maybe through new opportunities. Changes are made to correct problems, to infuse new methods, or even to redefine The Task. Change can affect any or all steps of the process.

The Organizational Design and Operating Process

What To Do

1. Envision A Need Or Possibility

2. Understand The Task

3. Identify Direct Processes To Do The Task

4. Identify Support Processes

5. Make A Process Organization Chart

6. Define And Set The Boundaries Of The Processes

7. Establish Process Methods

8. Develop Ground Rules For The Chart

9. Establish Rules For Everyone

10. Sequence & Schedule The Action

11. Identify What's Needed To Do This

Doing It

12. Find People

13. Empower The People

Watching/Improving/Changing

14. Watch

15. Fix/Improve/Re-plan

Remember, organizations are created to do something, to take action. Notice the descriptions of the steps are verbs, action verbs. They describe something that must be done. This is a more important point than it may appear. Organizations based on nouns, things or "lumps of people," lead to confusion, making it easy to forget that the foundation of an organization is The Task, doing something. Therefore, the Process Organization chart created in step 5 will be comprised of action verbs.

The process steps must be done in order. This is a sequential process. Do not, Do Not change the order or skip any of the steps. Start with step 1 and finish it before going to step 2, etc. And, half-hearted efforts on any one step put your organization at risk. I have seen billions of dollars wasted because management does not do this work, does not organize using this process. Disasters are borne of some nebulous vision, an attempt at step 1, which is immediately given a budget (step 11) and a schedule (step 10) without anyone really knowing what needs to happen (steps 2 through 9). It is absolutely unbelievable to witness. The confusion and waste are staggering. People are frustrated, become downright angry and the organization is a disaster. Organizations like this must have huge resources available to waste, or they will disappear.

Notice the first eleven steps do not mention the word "people." This follows directly from our earlier words about the importance of The Task; people come later. The Task comes first in an organization. Disasters start by throwing people into disorganized confusion that has no Task or plan. People want to help and be a part of something successful. And, they know that you can't be successful if you don't know what to do and at least have some plan for how it will be done.

Recognize the simplicity of each step. Remember, a complex subject is merely a series of simple steps. For instance, the first six steps may be summed up as "what we want to do." It takes six steps just to get to that point. Each step builds to an accurate, complete definition of The Task the organization wants to do. Steps seven through nine are "how we're gonna do it." Steps ten and eleven finish off planning the look and operation of the organization by defining an integrated schedule of actions each process will take and then identifying what's needed (equipment, money, people, etc.) to do them. So, the eleven steps of What To Do are the plan of what's going to happen, how it's going to happen, and when it's going to happen if our estimate of what it takes to do it shows that our idea is feasible. Yes, it's possible to come up with a brilliant, well-organized plan to manufacture golf balls but cost estimates of your plan may show your golf balls will be too expensive to sell. If you recognize this in time at least you haven't thrown a bunch of people and money into the organization before realizing this. You'll need to re-think your plan.

It may be hard to recognize, but there is a lot of work to do to complete these first eleven extremely important steps in sequential order. Do not skip or make light of any of the steps. Upon reaching step eleven a What To Do plan has been developed to get The Task done. A Process Organization Chart (step 5) will show The Task broken down into processes to do it. And, there will be a plan of how to do those processes (steps 7 and 8).

After the plan is made Doing It adds that important material—People. People will execute the plan. The organizational engineer uses the four Scientific Principles to support those people. Correctly and completely done, What To Do (steps 1 through 11) makes Doing It (steps 12 and 13) much easier. That's because having identified all the processes necessary to do The Task has defined the skills and knowledge needed in the people. Thus, it's easier to find the right people. Once the right people are on board they are empowered to do their process. Empowerment is a huge, important subject. It is the key to unleashing the power of the sun, the power of people. But, it must be done right. I have seen empowerment misunderstood, what a mess. We will explain empowerment later.

Now there is a living, breathing organization doing what it needs to do to accomplish The Task. The next thing to do is Watch/Improve/Change. There are some things to consider here. For instance, many people make a grave mistake in this area; they watch the wrong things, things that someone else should watch. A bunch of wasted motion goes into finding out the wrong stuff. It's like watching to see how well you're making fishing reels when you actually got into the business of making golf balls. That sounds pretty strange, but it happens. People watch the wrong things; they watch things that others should watch and don't watch what they should watch. We'll discuss how to watch in order to improve or change your organization.

So, The Organizational Design and Operating Process is a sequential method of first deciding what to do, figuring out how to do it, doing it, and then checking on how things are going and changing when it seems appropriate. All the steps are important.

Design
(Formerly "Management Planning")

A mechanical engineer designs the structure, the arrangement of a machine's parts to get it to do something, its Task. Likewise, the organizational engineer designs the structure of the organization so it can accomplish its Task.

The "Design" phase of organizational engineering is the first eleven steps of The Organizational Design and Operating Process: the "What To Do" steps.

What To Do

1. Envision A Need Or Possibility

2. Understand The Task

3. Identify Direct Processes To Do The Task

4. Identify Support Processes

5. Make A Process Organization Chart

6. Define And Set The Boundaries Of The Processes

7. Establish Process methods

8. Develop Ground Rules For The Chart

9. Establish Rules For Everyone

10. Sequence & Schedule The Action

11. Identify What's Needed To Do This

The first six steps are merely the "What" the organization is intended to do. Why six steps just to describe such a simple thing as "What" to do? Surprisingly, this is a much misunderstood, yet really basic necessity to success. It's amazing what little attention it is given, even when it entails millions or billions of dollars. I have seen hundreds of millions of dollars wasted and people's working lives made miserable because "What To Do" has been neglected. Hard to believe, but true.

Steps seven through eleven design "How" to do "What" the organization has chosen to do. Again, these are important considerations. They describe what our valuable materials, people, will do when they walk into work each day. (Or, what you and the neighbors will be doing in the project to clean-up the community park. Yes, Organizational Engineering isn't just for companies/businesses; it is the way to do anything efficiently.)

If the organization is to be efficient and productive these eleven steps must be done, in order. If the people that eventually operate the organization are to be happy, energetic and productive, steps one to eleven must be done, in order. As we describe some of the steps it will become apparent this is a "pay me now or pay me (a lot more) later" proposition. Design is that crucial beginning of organizational life. Skimping on design will cost later, big time. Make the effort; do the homework; take the time to design the organization right, the first time. No, it will not come out perfectly. Changes are inevitable. But, the first steps are important and your organization's success is entirely dependent on starting off in the right direction.

What To Do

Step 1—Envision a Need or Possibility

Years ago there was a business in San Francisco that sold ready-mixed concrete, delivered in those large trucks with the rotating barrel. The trucks were quite distinctive in their two-tone pink paint. On the side of the rotating barrel was a slogan: "find a need and fill it." Apparently, the vision was that San Francisco needed concrete. So, they charged in and became successful. There were many trucks, the outfit was there as long as I was; maybe it's still there because San Francisco is a busy place that probably needs lots of concrete.

There's actually more to this than meets the eye of the casual observer. Envisioning, envisioning fully, takes some effort. Some even hire this thing out to marketing consultants specializing in all the little details that may be involved in predicting the future of this vision. Or it may be as simple as: I have a dog, how big does my doghouse need to be? Have I a large or small dog? That concrete outfit even had to envision whether or not one more concrete supplier was needed in San Francisco. Was there a big enough market, big enough need for concrete for them to be successful? Could they operate such an organization competitively, beating the price and delivery experience of organizations already in the business? Should a company already involved in manufacturing snow skis decide to jump into the ready-mix concrete business? Do you need a doghouse at all, or does the dog live in the garage?

Visions need some kind of justification behind them. Those justifications are the "need" or the "possibility." Apparently that vision of the "possibility" to be successful in the concrete business was correct. They were there for years, and still may be there. Perhaps you don't need a doghouse of any size if the dog will live in the garage or house. If there is no "need", no "possibility," no reason for an organization to get in the concrete business, or for you to build a doghouse, don't start!

There is a trap here. I've seen it in big companies. The need or possibility gets lost in the shuffle. Something that isn't needed is done or else possibilities are missed. There are big companies that don't take the time to examine the need of a seemingly small project. Small projects get lost in the millions and billions of dollars of the annual budgets of big companies. Billions are lost, wasted on unneeded projects because no one running the outfit spends the time to discuss the need with those asking for the budget to do something. Yes, big companies are kind of like the federal government; they have money to waste. Pork barrel projects get smothered in the vast budgetary process.

Basically, two things result from this waste that's caused by people not properly envisioning the need. First, and the most obvious result in the short-term, annual budgets become bloated, one little bit at a time. I believe it was some decades ago when former Senator Dirksen said something like: "a billion here a billion there; pretty soon you're talking real money." The federal budget is loaded with unnecessary, pork barrel projects. Money is spent for no really good reason, spent just for political gain. Eventually, organizations die from budgetary, "visionary" stupidity. While the government may be able to afford this kind of crazy spending, private profit-making enterprise (and you and I) cannot. This wasteful environment leads to the second result of this lack of visionary oversight by organizations. This is a long-term process leading to the death of organizations. This kind of uncontrolled "vision" leading to useless projects instills a lethal attitude in the organization. Remember, people make up organizations. And, when these people see the stupidity in charge of the organization their attitude changes. "The boss doesn't care about what happens, so why should I?" Sound unreal? Well, it is real! This stuff happens. The only organization that can continue living with this kind of attitude is the one with no competition, one whose customers pay exorbitant prices for their product or service, one with customers who are willing to pay "cost plus." The government is the perfect example. Some very lucky, private, for-profit companies are also in this ballgame. But, on the whole, most organizations aren't in this situation. They've got to do the right thing, efficiently and without waste.

I've got a brother who is some kind of big shot in a national consulting engineering firm. Engineering consultants are in the business of designing the details of machines and structures, things that do something. So, you'd think that his firm spends its time specifying how something should be built, what materials will be used, etc. Well, he told me that they spend about 90% of their time and effort just trying to find out what their customer wants/needs/envisions. This is a huge concept. Think of the waste caused if someone doesn't spend all the time that's required to envision what is needed or possible. I want a doghouse. Go! So you build a doghouse to suit any dog, maybe not your dog. Money is wasted; the dog doesn't fit or doesn't like it. Strange example? Well, this happens in big, brilliant(?), well-respected companies. Billions of dollars are wasted on un-needed stuff because the management doesn't do what they should do. It doesn't spend enough effort to review its need or possibility.

So, take the time. Think awhile. Envision your need or possibility. Write it down. Write down some details about it. Define your vision so that someone without your vision can also visualize what you're thinking. Think about that defined vision. Does it seem necessary or have a good chance to be a future reality, a fantastic possibility?

Step 2—Understand The Task

That engineering firm spends 90% of its effort just trying to figure out what the customer needs or wants. All that work, all that money spent just to get the idea of what's needed to be done. The next step is to translate that vision into reality. How does that vision blossom into something that is real, something that can happen? This is where the rubber meets the road. How does fantasy, the vision, become reality, The Task? We must Understand The Task.

I once went through an exercise with a department in a big company. This department had been operating for decades. We got onto this subject of The Task. At first those managing the department said they did just one thing, one basic Task. And, they thought they were organized to do it, but they were having some problems. Somehow they felt like something was missing; things were not going as smoothly as they thought they should be. After talking with them for just one hour it was recognized that their vision of what they were suppose to be doing did not match The Task they were organized to do. In fact their vision actually was made up of seven elements, not just the one that was their Task. They were not organized or operating to do the seven elements. They were missing something—The Task was not understood. Amazing, decades of operating while not understanding The Task and, therefore, not set up to do it. We had to go back to step one to define the vision, then do step 2 to Understand The Task. Remember: **You cannot Understand The Task if you have not fully defined The Vision**. Step 1 must be complete before step 2.

Another story. Years ago I was hustled into a discussion with a group of thirty or so people. It turned out they were all involved in a project to help part of their company improve its operations. The project had been going on for about three months; they had spent several hundred thousand dollars. The manager who dragged me into the discussion had something to do with one part of the project; the rest of the people were from other departments, all involved in the project. Things were not going well. The three months, the dollars were almost a total waste: time and money down the drain. After ten minutes of discussion it was easy to see that all these people in all these separate groups didn't actually know what they needed to do; they did not Understand The Task, in detail. The project was started over. It started with step 1, Envisioning The Need, to make sure everyone was on the same page and that they were all there to get the same thing done. (Remember Scientific Principle number one?) Then, The Task was defined and written down so everyone understood it. Two things happened: the job got done, and the people became more productive by learning that Understanding The Task is the key to starting a project, any project.

A most telling experience about this Understanding The Task was in the rebuilding of an organization, an organization that was in trouble. Due to several reasons—all a result of not using the Scientific Principles—it was not doing its Task. Top management was not happy with the situation. So, the management staff of the department was replaced. The next six months were spent just concentrating on the business at hand, the department's assigned Task. No attention was given to results: no measures of performance were made. Everyone just worked on doing The Task. Processes were changed. People did different things. Things began to really pop. Significant benefits were gained just because everyone started by Understanding The Task. There were actually several elements to The Task, and everyone knew them. The Task was accomplished because the Scientific Principles were used and people Understood The Task. After one year top management said that the worst department in the plant had become the best.

The Task is either making something, or providing a service. Step 2 says figure out what you have to make or do. It's quite a simple idea. However, even as simple as it sounds some people get mixed up. It is really easy to get stuck on "making money." Yes, it's true that most organizations must take in money, but making money is not the thing, The Task, that the organization does, unless it's the U.S. mint. The organization does something that is worthwhile; it provides a need or (valued) possibility. The Task is not making money. "Making money" does not say what is to be done to make the money. Try telling people in an organization: "We're going to make money." Their return: "So, what are we going to do to make money?" They will want to know what they will do each day they walk into work. Are we going to make golf balls or rocket ships, or fix ships or sell insurance? The Task may be written as something like this: "We are going to manufacture, package, sell and ship golf balls to retail sporting goods stores." That's something people can understand.

Some finance types have really gotten on my case about this "forget the money" thing. Some years ago I went to a university graduation exercise. The keynote speaker was a very successful gentleman, experienced in bringing back big businesses from fatal situations. The title of his speech was: "Don't do it for the money." The gist was: do something worthwhile, a Task, and do it well; the money will come.

There are lots of fine ideas I've heard about this Task business. There are "mission statements" (Task statements?) that say things like "be the customers' preferred supplier", or "make the customer happy." These are fine ideas, but they are only conditions you would like to reach. They are just like "making money." They are not what you are going to do for the customer. Leave all those nice words out when you are writing down your Task. The Task to write down tells exactly what you're going to do to make money and make the customer happy. This short discussion will talk about a golf ball factory. If golf balls are needed and if we do it efficiently, better than other golf ball makers, we will make the customers happy and make money, automatically. All the good stuff naturally flows out of the fact that we've done our Task very well.

Understand The Task ties in directly with step 1. It may seem obvious that our prediction of a future need or possibility must guide our Task, but it is surprisingly easy to get lost from step 1 to step 2. It can be confusing to convert "what we envision happening" to "what we're going to do." Be very careful when doing this step. Make sure The Task written down and understood comes directly from the "vision."

Understand The Task, the specific task. Are we going to make several models of golf balls? Are we going to make 100,000 balls a year or 100,000,000? Write it down. Consider Scientific Principle number one; get everyone behind the effort to do it.

Step 3—Identify Direct Processes to Do The Task

We have just spent a lot of effort to make sure everyone Understands The Task, completely. That's 90% of the work to get something done? Things now fall into place simply because we now know what needs to be done. Warning: if we did not do Step 2, and spend the time to do it very well, we'd have trouble from here on. The rest of the steps would be much more difficult, if not impossible. Now it's time to Identify Direct Processes to Do The Task.

The Task is now going to be broken down into processes, sub-Tasks if you wish, which must happen to do The Task. We are going to call these processes Direct Processes because they directly do The Task. This step is a perfect example of the simplicity of the organizational design process. The Direct Processes are already introduced in our definition of The Task. This is so obvious and easy that sometimes people don't understand how Organizational Engineering can be so effective because it seems too simple.

We could start a brand new organization, but let's say we are already in the golf ball manufacturing business and we're having difficulty doing our Task. (It seems to me that this is the case with most organizations these days.) Everyone from the boss down knows the place doesn't run well. People are frustrated. A lot of golf balls are scrapped because production doesn't run well. Customers complain about slow delivery, incorrect billing, and promises about the quality of the balls don't seem to be true. We are continually re-organizing. Everything's a mess.

Enter the organizational design process and the scientific principles. After much discussion everyone finally agrees with the vision from Step 1 and now Understand The Task to be: make, package, sell and ship golf balls to retail stores in the western United States. While our example is defined in simple terms, remember that in reality there will be some details, like numbers of golf balls to be made and maybe specific places we'll market our golf balls. Defining The Task in real situations takes time. Take some time; it's worth it. We're not going to do it here; enough said, just make sure you know what you want to do. Step 2 makes you define The Task, specifically.

We are now ready to Identify Direct Processes to Do The Task. For instance, making the golf balls may be one of the processes. Or "Make" could be broken down into several other processes like: obtain specifications for making golf balls, buy and check materials, operate the golf ball making machine(s), check your product (golf ball quality control?), transport the balls to the packaging area, etc. How far we go on this process identification depends upon many factors like volume of business, geographic considerations, etc. There is nothing wrong with being very specific or staying rather general as long as we do the rest of the steps to suit the option we pick. However, I would recommend that a good start would be very general processes like option A rather than B. But, it's up to you.

Option "A" Direct Processes:	Make Golf Balls
	Package Golf Balls
	Sell Golf Balls
	Ship Golf Balls
Option "B" Direct Processes:	Buy Material and Specifications
	Inspect Material
	Make Golf Balls
	Check Golf Balls
	Package Golf Balls
	Sell Golf Balls
	Ship Golf Balls

Both options A and B are merely a breakout of the definition of The Task. Step 3 is quite simple. Option "B" just breaks down "make" into more direct processes than "A". It may be as simple as separating the action verbs in The Task definition, from Step 2, into Direct Processes; that's what option A does. Direct Processes are developed from the Task definition. This makes us stick to The Task.

Step 4—Identify Support Processes

We've just listed the Direct Processes to do The Task. There are also some other processes, other things to do to run an operation: things that must happen to help our Direct Processes do The Task. These other processes play an important supporting role; these are Support Processes because they support the Direct Processes.

For example, an organization usually needs some kind of facilities support and accounting services. To do almost anything some kind of space and equipment is needed. If we are going to make golf balls, we'll need: a building, one or more golf ball making machines, some offices, packing/shipping area, utilities, restrooms, office equipment, etc. The accounting support process may be described as: "Record and Report Financial Activities". Note the generality of that process title. In this step all we're doing is just recognizing that this process is needed. Details will come later. Also note the process title/description starts with action verbs. Something is to be done.

So, in step 4 we identify those kinds of things we need to do to support the Direct Processes. This does not mean that Support Processes are any less valuable than the Direct Processes. Try getting fifty people to work at a place without a restroom. It is easy to see that restrooms are a fairly important support need. We need a process that provides and maintains restrooms. And, in some cases, the support people you'll need may have higher qualifications, more skills than the Direct Process people. It may take more skill to repair and maintain complicated golf ball machines than to operate them, much like an automobile. Support Processes are just as necessary as the Direct Processes and must be a part of the plan.

But, there is an important point here. Support Processes should not decide how Direct Processes are to operate. Support needs are important; otherwise they would not be included. And, some of the support needs require a lot of skill to do. But, support people do not make decisions on how the Direct Processes do their work, any part of their work. Remember our story of the personnel department that shut down changes on the production floor? This error is disastrous. Rule 2 is destroyed. The Direct Processes are not controlling their methods; someone else is. (Actually they're not controlling them; they are destroying them.) Direct Processes must control themselves.

The personnel department is not the only Support Process that can try to dictate to Direct Processes. Given the chance any Support Process can be the culprit. I've seen finance and facilities processes have similar influence—always a disaster. An accounting system must be set up to watch the extent of your resources being used to do your Direct Processes. But, do not let the accountants take over the reins of the operation. Don't let Support Processes attempt to control Direct Processes. The essence of the organization is the Direct Process work because they are doing The Task. The Direct Processes are The Task.

We meet an important point, a very important point. There is something more than just knowing Scientific Principles and The Organizational Design and

Operating Process. Yes, we've got to go with them, but there must be some intelligent "feel" to what we are doing. I recently left a huge, uncontrolled monster of an organization. There is apparently no one who knows how to structure and operate a single project or a continuing organization. The method used to manufacture their product reminds me of a saying: "Give an infinite number of monkeys and infinite number of typewriters and they will produce all of Shakespeare's works." Don't get me wrong; I'm not calling all of the talented production people monkeys. The point is that the lack of competent management has resulted in a very confused, unproductive environment. This requires an unbelievable amount of resources to manufacture their product. Fortunately for them, there is no real competition in their business and customers continue to pay huge prices for their products. One part of the problem is that they have more support things going on than necessary. More effort and money is spent on support processes than is necessary. They have more non-value added things going on than value-added things. The whole thing just didn't "feel" right when you watched all the "non-Task", administrative stuff going on. Do not get carried away with Support Processes. Support is necessary to help the direct processes, not to take their place. If there is a problem in getting a Direct Process to do its Task, fix that Direct Process. Do not add another Process, Support or Direct, to take its place. This is deadly. Fix your Direct Process if it's not working. This may sound stupid, but I've seen it. I have seen four separate departments set up to do the same thing, in the same place. Talk about confusion, jurisdictional disputes and waste.

Support Processes are needed, but they must be kept to a minimum and know their supporting role.

Step 5—Make a Process Organization Chart

Now that we have taken the time to fully Understand The Task and have identified both the Direct and Support Processes, it is time to make a Process Organization Chart. Step 5 consists merely of making a graphical depiction of The Task and the Direct and Support Processes. This is not complicated at all. Optional process organizations "A" and "B" are shown on page 27. In the charts the Direct Processes are linked to the Task with solid lines, the Support Processes with dotted lines.

These organizations look awfully simple. How can they be of any help? That's just the point; simplicity is understandable, simplicity is flexible, simplicity is doable while complexity is not. Of course we have not included all the things necessary to set up a factory. It does take longer than a few pages to set up a whole organization. We'll show a more elaborate organization chart later. But, these few steps are actually just as simple as they seem. The chart summarizes the first four steps in a graphic way. And, to repeat for emphasis, note that each Process, both Direct and Support, starts with an action verb; each Process must do something.

The Organizational Engineering system is not just a recipe for changing or building an organization. It is an evolutionary thought process. So far, a lot of thinking has been done, but very little black and white writing. Steps 1 through 4 are done simply. They are only meant to force you to think, in a logical manner. Step 5 is a snapshot of all that thinking. This is an excellent time to sit back and stare at the results. Is this really what you want to do? Is The Task really the "vision" from step 1? Is The Task fully defined? Remember the story about the group that actually had seven elements to its Task but had only recognized one; they stumbled along for years. Are all the Direct and Support Processes identified and shown on the chart? Think!

It is probable that your initial shot at doing these first steps will not include everything. Just do the best you can. You'll find that later steps will help you catch anything missing.

It is theoretically possible for one person to sit in the corner and do these first five steps all by themselves, building an organization. And, if you're going to do your own project or start your own business, that's what you should do, the steps. But, if you're talking about re-organizing an existing project or business, everyone should be involved. The Scientific Principles play a key role in achieving success.

Process Organization Charts

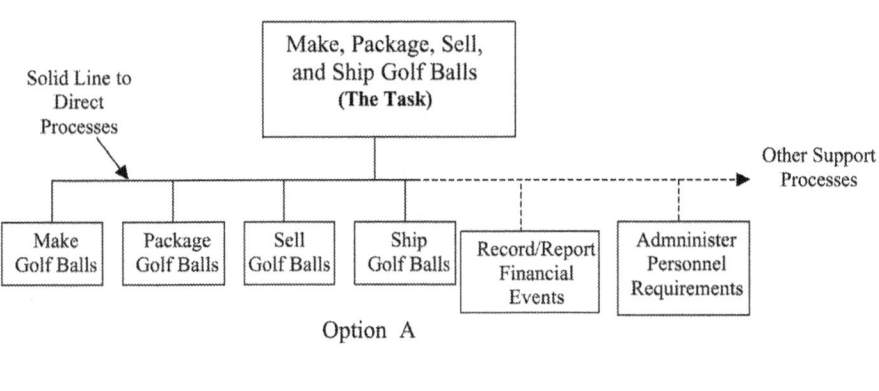

Option A

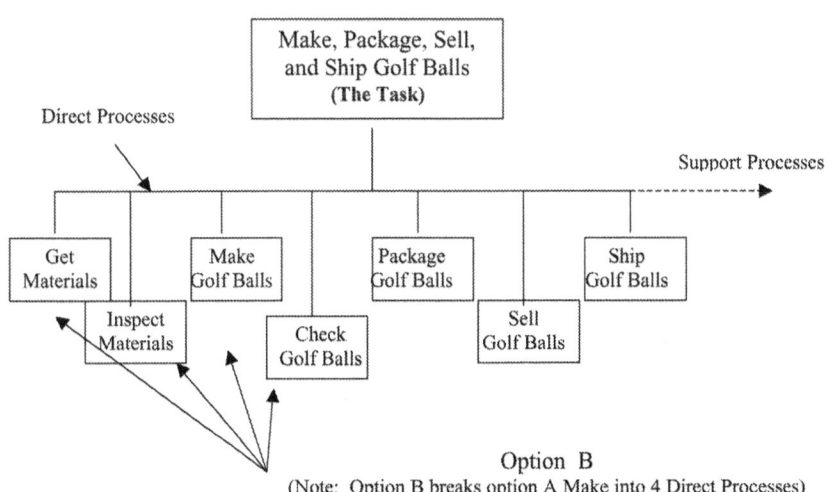

Option B
(Note: Option B breaks option A Make into 4 Direct Processes)

Step 6—Define and Set the Boundaries of The Processes

Step 6 is a detailed development of steps 3 and 4. The few short words used to identify the Processes in those steps will be expanded. Someday someone is going to actually do the Processes, and they will need a clear, complete picture of what is to be done.

For example, one of our golf ball company's option A Processes is "Make the Golf Balls." A definition of this Process may go something like: "Make The Golf Balls will acquire golf ball design specifications, materials, production procedures, equipment and personnel to produce golf balls as directed by Sell The Golf Balls, and deliver them to Package The Golf Balls."

Important—Step 6 defines what that box on the chart is going to do, not how it will be done. Let's be clear on that. Step 6 says to define what the Processes are to do, not how. We're doing one simple step at a time. Don't get hung up with a lot of complications during any one step. Step 6 is a challenge anyway without trying to think of too much at one time. The series of steps will develop all the details. Notice that we set the boundaries when defining each Process: "...deliver them to Package..." limits the Make Process. Another process, not Make, will handle and box the golf balls. In addition, Sell The Golf Balls will be defined as providing the quantity and type of balls to be made.

Package's process may be defined something like: "Package The Golf Balls will receive all golf balls from Make, acquire packaging materials and package (including application of address labels) golf balls per directions from Sell The Golf Balls, then deliver them to Ship The Golf Balls." Again, the definition of Package's process says what it's going to do and what its limits are. Its work comes from Make and Sell; then it hands its product, packaged golf balls, to Ship The Golf Balls. So, Package has nothing to do with actually manufacturing golf balls, nor does it deal with customers. Make and Sell do those Processes.

When all the Processes have been defined and their boundaries are set, they "touch" each other. The common boundaries between Make, Package, Sell, Ship and any other Processes are apparent.

After defining all the Processes, including the Support Processes, they must add up to everything needed to do The Task. There are problems to look for here: gaps and overlaps in the Process definitions. Gaps are easy to spot. Once the work begins something that obviously needs to be done doesn't get done. Gaps are readily apparent. Unfortunately, overlaps can be more difficult to spot and can become a fatal flaw in your organization. I've seen organizations with two, three, even four different departments (processes on the chart) doing the same work. Seem like a good idea? At least everything is getting done. Bad idea! When people in different processes find out that someone else is also doing the same work either no one does it or everything gets really confused because they all do it, differently. The work stumbles along with holes in it, or confusion reigns because several people are doing the same thing in different ways. This happens; what a mess. Costs skyrocket. The Task suffers.

However, all is not lost because later steps will help us. Both gaps and overlaps can be quickly seen because the organizational engineer watches, in Step 14, the Processes and their interaction using the Ground Rules established in Step 8. We're getting there.

We have traveled through almost half the Steps. Yet all we've talked about is <u>what</u> we're going to do. You would think that establishing an organization would be a lot, lot more than just trying to figure out and understand what you're going to do. Think of all the things to be done, watched, and changed while the organization operates. Yes, there is much left to do. But, you are now seeing what it takes to make sure we do not fall into that lethal, confusing trap: not knowing what we're trying to do. It is amazingly simple to get into real trouble by not doing Steps 1 through 6 completely. Remember the engineering firm that spends 90% of their time trying to find out just what the customer wants or needs. Do not, do not slight any of these steps. If you do there will be fireworks down the road. Having seen hundreds of millions of dollars wasted from just such confusion, I can guarantee that if you do not know what you are going to do, or do not let everyone else know, life will be very exciting, too exciting.

Step 7—Establish Process Methods

Now that The Task is understood and the Processes have been well defined, it's time to decide how to do the Processes. Step 6 defined "what" the Processes are going to do; now it's time to decide "how" we're going to do them.

Take our Ship The Golf Balls Process, which was defined in step 6. We can decide to either, buy our own trucks and hire drivers to deliver the balls, or to contract a trucking firm. Each of those methods takes somewhat different actions and resources to get them done. That's why how to deliver the balls must be decided. Think about the details, like how many balls and how often we want to deliver to our customers. Make a decision, write it down, review it, and move on. Upcoming steps include watching the methods we've chosen; watching will lead to changes and improvements as we see fit.

The description of how each Process will be done also specifies how it interacts with the other Processes. For instance, somewhere in Make The Golf Balls method it should be stated how it will receive orders from Sell The Golf Balls, say by some paper form or maybe an electronic message, etc., and how it will deliver its products, the balls, to the next process, Package. These interactions are an extremely important part of the operation. In fact, coordinating the Processes is so important we will be emphasizing it in step 8.

We may bump into a serious problem, which is currently growing at a fast pace these days, in this step, especially for big organizations. The problem is "procedures." There are corporate procedures, divisional procedures, departmental procedures, and on and on. It takes a lot of time and effort to build them. They are written in long, tedious documents which tend to be written in complicated semi-legalese wording and, most importantly, they are not used to do the Processes. People doing the productive work don't have time to sift through them every day. Formal procedures sit in a pile of dust on the shelf or buried in a computer. But, the most lethal aspect of these formal procedures is that they can become very stiff, inflexible to the point of strangling execution of the Processes. They can stifle that power of the sun in people, trashing their creativity and ability to perform. Detailed procedures cannot possibly cover all situations that arise in doing something; there is always that unanticipated situation that comes along that is not quite covered by the procedure. Any organization that is run strictly by the procedure book gives people the idea that they cannot do something if it isn't an officially approved procedure, even if it makes sense to do. Creativity and brainpower are destroyed—the death of common sense. Rule 2 is destroyed. People are not controlling their own Processes; someone else is, someone who writes procedures.

Why does this seem to be such a serious problem? Because I've seen the damage done. Yet, unfortunately, business must have formal documents to get along in this regulated and litigious world. You can't conduct business these days using just simple, logical common sense. Even outstandingly productive organizations must contend with the confusion and complexity of today's legal/regulated industry. Sometimes formally written procedures are needed to back up decisions, or just put up a good image.

Be that as it may, in the real world at the working level of organizations, where the Task is performed, people need short, concise, logical words to say how they're going to do their Processes. Process methods are to be written in everyday, layman words to insure the work, The Task, gets done with minimum of waste, confusion, and frustration. For each Process write, in layman's words, the method to be used to perform that Process.

Step 8—Develop Ground Rules for The Chart.

So far we've got: The Task, The Processes, a Process Organization chart, definitions of what each Process does, and methods to do the Processes simply described. Now we've got to make sure that the Processes communicate with each other so that the individual Processes work together to do The Task. This is the key to the organizational engineer's job—conducting the orchestra of Processes so they work together to make a symphony, not a confused and noisy mess.

Ground Rules define how the different Processes in the boxes on the chart are going to work together to get The Task done. For instance, our option B organization has a Process called Check the Golf Balls (quality control?). A Ground Rule may say: "If Check the Golf Balls finds that 3 % of the golf balls produced in any one hour of production are rejects according to specifications, they will inform Make the Golf Balls to stop production." There may be additional details like "use Form XYZ and record the problem in the quality control logbook." This is a Ground Rule on how Check will interact with Make. There should be another Ground Rule on how Check and Make will get together to remedy the situation.

Our Processes defined in step 6 and Process Methods of step 7 must mesh with these Ground Rules. Process definitions and methods should already include the way Processes talk to each other. This step just emphasizes them to make sure everyone recognizes these interactions between Processes. It may seem redundant to rewrite something that already exists in other steps, but these Ground Rules are so important we must make sure they are very visible and seen as a major part of the total operation of the organization. And, later you'll see how the Ground Rules are a major part of the Watching the organizational engineer must do while conducting the orchestra of Processes.

What if we don't establish and make these Ground Rules easily visible? Imagine a football huddle in which no one tells anyone what he should do in the next play. When the quarterback steps back to throw a pass he expects the receivers to go downfield for a pass, not block for a runner. Chaos! Things get confused, expensive, hard to do. The Task suffers. In our example, Make would keep wasting time and money producing golf balls that go in the trashcan. (Unfortunately, most of the problems caused by poor or no interaction between Processes can be more subtle than a visible, growing pile of trashed golf balls.) Without Ground

Rules the Processes become isolated from each other. Both The Task and the people suffer. But again, all is not lost if the organizational engineer does the Watching he/she is suppose to do. We will be discussing that in steps 14 and 15.

So, Develop Ground Rules for the Chart and make sure everyone knows them. Later it will be the organizational engineer's responsibility to be sure that the Ground Rules are followed and are appropriate for coordinating the operations of the Processes.

Step 9—Establish Rules for Everyone

Okay, we've got a real Process Organization plan. We know what we've got to do (steps 1 through 6) and how we're going to do it (steps 7 and 8). We now create some generic rules under which to operate: things that affect everyone in their day-to-day work. While these rules are not directly connected to doing the Processes like the Ground Rules, they are important support rules. Some people call these support rules "policies."

Rules for Everyone are just that. Everyone in the organization will abide by them. These rules usually start out with basics: attendance rules, compliance with any laws, mandating a certain kind of accounting procedure, perhaps a bonus system based on say a person's performance and/or the organizations profits, etc. These rules are quite important. Think of them as the foundation for operating and living in a civilized, efficient organization.

Important point—these Rules for Everyone must be applied consistently, across the board to everyone, and not side-stepped. This is a warning: big trouble starts when one of these rules (say, an attendance rule) is not applied consistently. Organizations, and their bosses, encounter big trouble when the rule is not applied objectively, to all people. People's attitudes, and therefore performance, go right down the tubes. The boss is seen to be "playing favorites." Make these Rules. Apply these Rules, consistently.

Step 10—Sequence & Schedule the Action

Now that we know what is to happen (steps 1 through 6) and how it is to happen (steps 7 through 9), it's time to think about "when" it will happen. A schedule is made for each Process, both direct and support; then the individual Process schedules are combined to schedule the whole effort, The Task.

The Process schedules are constructed by first sequencing each activity it takes to do the process. Sequencing is merely laying out the logical steps needed to activate the process. In order to erect walls on a new house it is necessary to first build the foundation and flooring. So, erecting the house structure may be sequenced as: foundation, then flooring, then walls, then roof trusses, then roofing. Each step of the sequence is then allotted some estimated time to complete. That could be: foundation 4 days, flooring 3 days, walls 5 days, roof trusses 3 days, roofing 3 days. In this case each step is done in order, one after the other. Some steps may be done concurrently. The plumbers may install piping at the same time electricians are installing wiring and the power panel.

There are lots of scheduling formats these days. Many computer options are available. As crude as it may sound, some people still prefer an old fashioned, manual method. It makes them think, giving them time to consider their steps and estimated times to do each step. Sometimes faster is not better.

No matter the scheduling method used, there is one thing common to all of them: they all need good work done on the preceding design steps (1 through 9). Again, how can we schedule something if we don't know what it is or how we're going to do it? Do not just throw some dates at The Task. I've seen that happen; it causes some very tense and expensive situations once the work is underway.

There is some linkage between this step and the next: schedules can be influenced by the resources, money, People, etc., required to do The Processes.

Step 11—Identify What's Needed To Do This

Yes, step 11 is a relative to step 10, and it is the last step in What To Do. Just like scheduling, this takes more than just looking at The Task and throwing a bucket of money or whatever at it. What's needed to do the whole Task is made up of what's needed to do each Process. And, just like step 10, there is no way to do this step if we have not done all the preceding steps. We must decide whether we're going to buy a delivery truck and hire a driver for "Ship Golf Balls" or just contract a trucking company. We must know what and how we're going to do the Processes before allotting resources to do them.

Steps 10 and 11 are somewhat related because it is possible to accelerate a schedule by tossing in more money and energy. If we want our golf ball factory fast, we work the construction crew on overtime or pay a premium to the golf ball machine maker to deliver quickly.

Keep in mind that money, even gross amounts of money, can't buy everything. It is possible that you crystal-balled doing something but the resources, brains, or equipment are not available at any cost. Money won't get it. If you need a turbo-charged rocket scientist to do a Process but they are all kept in caves doing secret work for the government, your plan won't fly.

Steps 1 through 11

Okay folks, now it's time to stop and look. We've made it all the way through What To Do. This is "THE PLAN." Is our vision of a need or possibility reality or fantasy? Does The Task we understand (step 2) make sure the vision will happen? Does the whole plan make sense? Are all the Processes identified (step 3 and 4)? Are they well defined (step 6)? Do we know how we're going to do each process (step 7)? Are all the processes "talking" to each other (step 8 ground rules)? Does it make financial sense? Are golf balls going to cost $10 a piece to make but potential customers already get a decent ball for a buck. Is the plan realistic?

The next four steps depend upon how well we've done the first eleven steps. You are now about to commit resources like people and money to this plan. **Stop! Think! Talk to the people around you, if you have any. Get everyone involved.**

A cartoon I saw years ago shows a man walking through a group of people sitting at desk, obviously a department of a large corporation. He's saying something like: "We've been given a schedule and a budget. You make up a schedule chart and cost detail. I'll go find out what the project is about." The people at the desks have confusion and amazement written all over their faces; they don't know how anyone can put a budget and timetable on a project that does not have a well-defined Task, nor any identified Processes to do The Task. As ridiculous as this sounds, it happens. I've seen literally billions of dollars wasted this way, wasted on projects started without a plan. The cartoon has a message: do steps one through eleven, do them in sequence, and do not skip or take any of them lightly.

What To Do

Step 1—Envision A Need Or Possibility

Step 2—Understand The Task

Step 3—Identify Direct Processes To Do The Task

Step 4—Identify Support Processes

Step 5—Make A Process Organization Chart

Step 6—Define and Set The Boundaries Of The Processes

Step 7—Establish Process Methods

Step 8—Develop Ground Rules For The Chart

Step 9—Establish Rules For Everyone

Step 10—Sequence and Schedule The Action

Step 11—Identify What's Needed To Do This

No physical work has happened yet. No one has started doing anything. Don't hire Fred to build a deck on the back of your house if you don't know where it's going, how big it should be, what it should look like. Figure these out then think about when you need it and how much (money?) your vision will take to do. Fred comes next.

Operating

An old saying: "Are we going to fish or just cut bait?" We can't fish without bait. We can't start doing something without knowing what we want to do. That's why we did Steps 1 through 11, What To Do, so thoroughly. We've prepared bait, our organizational design. Now it's time to fish, time to operate.

Steps 12 and 13, Doing It, both have the word People in them. People are the power of the sun waiting to be used. People, the potential energy which insures a thriving enterprise be it building a deck on the back of the house, making rocket ships, fixing ships, or running a school system. Our design will become a living, breathing organization.

Steps 14 and 15 (Watching/Improving/Changing) are the crucial final steps in Organizational Engineering. The organizational engineer will be watching the plan established by the What To Do steps. Not by any stretch of the imagination is the organizational engineer finished. Steps 14 and 15 start the continuous cycle of change, improvement and development of The Task, the Processes, the methods and people. Organizational Engineering is a constant, continuous activity that may affect any of the steps, even the Vision of step 1.

Doing It

Step 12—Find People

Finding people to do the Processes can be a very complex issue, full of worry, frustration, and risk. But, we have simplified the complex. Whether setting up a new organization or fixing one that's got some problems, Finding People is now simple. It is simple because the What To Do plan, steps 1 through 11, states what is to be done and how we're going to start doing it.

To begin, job descriptions, what people are going to do, already exist. The Process definitions and methods, steps 6 and 7, are job descriptions. They describe the work to be done and how we propose to do it. We may change some of this later, but for now we've got a plan. All we need to do is make sure the people know the plan.

The normal stuff happens in this step: applications, resumes, discussions and interviews. However, there is one subject we must talk about. Some people make the false assumption that someone applying for a job is at a disadvantage, asking for something, on the begging end, in need of a job. That is short-term thinking. In the long term, this is not really the case. People need a place that allows their dignity and their abilities to grow and flourish. An applicant is just as interested in getting the right job as we are in making this organization successful. Finding People is actually a two-way street. We are just as desperate to make this thing work as the applicant. Everyone has something at stake. While we are trying to Find People, people are trying to find someplace that needs their abilities and that operates in a fashion that allows them to use their skills. They want to help; we need help. They don't want to be trapped inside some confused, poorly run organization; we don't want the wrong people in the Processes. So, both parties are trying to fill their needs. No one really wants the wrong job, and no one really wants someone in the wrong job.

I once inherited a department. It was in serious need of help, but there were a lot of capable people in it. There was one fellow who was an adequate but just mediocre performer. He had the skills but not the heart to do the job. He was stuck, just working for a living. After many talks both he and I decided that he should look for something far different than he was doing. He left. I heard from him months later. He had found his place in the sun, doing his thing. His replacement was selected using the Organizational Engineering philosophy. Everyone benefited.

With this in mind, how do we Find People? After the normal course of advertising and applications we start talking. This talking is based on our What To Do: The Task and the Processes. So, the ball is in our court first. The organizational engineer must explain the whole plan. This is important; it gets everyone on the same wavelength. It follows the concept that the organization exists to do something; the something is now explained. The applicant must know right up front what the future is to be, what's going to happen, and how. During the discussion the applicant's feelings about The Task and the Processes start to surface. Something big has started—communication.

The applicant now has a fair idea of the job and how the surroundings will be. Everyone gets comfortable. The discussion moves into how well the background and interests of the applicant fit into this What To Do plan. What has happened? It is now possible for everyone to be honest about his/her position. The applicant feels comfortable because the organization has laid its cards on the table. That has eased the way for him/her to show his/her hand. We will find the right people.

The standard thinking is that the boss, the leader of the pack, finds people. Consider an alternative. Who better to find someone to do one of the Processes than someone already doing the Process? If the Scientific Principles and the

Design and Operating Process have been used to establish and operate the organization, you already have knowledgeable, motivated people in the Process. They are in the best position to Find People for their Process. This is merely a simple example of Principle 2 in action; you are allowing those doing a process to control their destiny. I have had mechanics hire their co-workers, even in union shops; it worked amazingly well.

So, Find People is a simple exercise because of our What To Do plan, and our use of the Scientific Principles.

Step 13—Empower The People

This is a huge step, an important subject. It is even more important than Find People. Even if we get perfectly qualified people for the Processes, we must create the best situation for them to succeed, to use their potential energy and skills. We must make sure that the sun shines brightly on our organization by applying the Scientific Principles. People become knowledgeable (Principle 3) and control their own Processes (Principle 2) that they help formulate (Principle 4). And, we have found the right people: people who want to do The Task (Principle 1).

We now have a well-defined Task, Processes, Ground Rules and people. Next is the key to success: Empowerment, which can be illustrated by the Empowerment Triangle. All good scouts know the Fire Triangle. The three legs of the fire triangle are oxygen, fuel and heat. If any one of the legs is missing, there's no fire. Hot fuel with no oxygen equals no fire. Hot oxygen with no fuel equals no fire. The three legs of the Empowerment Triangle are the Processes (Direct and Support), the Authority and the Knowledge to use that authority intelligently. If any one of the legs is missing, empowerment is not really happening.

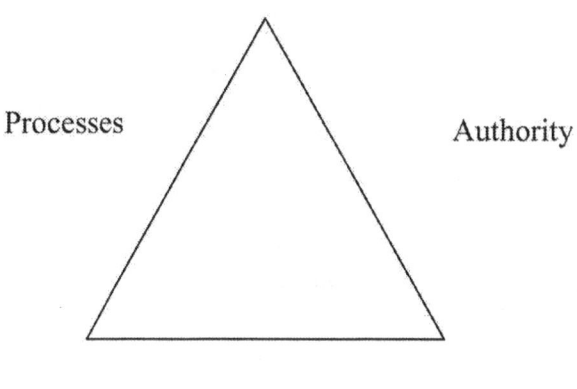

As simple as it looks, empowerment is often misunderstood. Not all of the legs are recognized, or not enough effort is put into making sure that all of the legs are completely executed. Organizations that do not define The Task well have no Processes. No Processes, no empowerment. Authority must be delegated to the people to do the Processes, giving them the power to act. No authority, no empowerment. The last leg is tricky. Scientific Principle 3 is very important here. Knowledge, gained through communication and information, is the key to this last leg. You are not empowering someone by giving them the authority to do something if they don't know how to do it. Giving the authority to uninformed people is dangerous. Problems are sure to arise. And, those problems are not their fault; they were told to do something and given the power to do it without possessing the skills or knowledge to do it right. The organizational engineer must be deeply involved in developing the knowledge and skills of the people. An organization's success depends on the knowledge, the competence of its people. So, all three legs of the empowerment triangle are to be executed clearly and completely.

Time to re-emphasize an important point—what is not delegated to the Process people, what they are not empowered to do. Organizational Engineering is not delegated to the Process people. Organizational engineers do Organizational Engineering. Process people do the productive work. The engineer executes The Design and Operating work while applying the Scientific Principles. The boss has work to do, Organizational Engineering. The Process people have work to do, the productive Processes. This is key. I have seen managers try to delegate their work. What a mess; things don't happen. The organization is not successful. Turmoil, confusion, frustration are rampant.

Does this seem contradictory to Principle 4: giving people the chance to help decide how to do something? Step 7 is the How to get the Processes done. Doesn't Principle 4 say that the people, not just the engineer, decide how to get the Processes done? Yes, the people help decide, but the final decisions on all the steps, including Step 7, are made by the engineer. That's why the engineer must be around; football coaches must stay with the team on the playing field. The organizational engineer sets up the Process Organization then finds people to do the Processes. With full participation of the engineer, the people help develop and change the methods to get the Processes done. Through the Scientific Principles people are helping the engineer do the steps, all of them. In reality, everyone is involved in Organizational Engineering. But, the boss is the boss.

Empower people properly; remember the Empowerment Triangle. Have them participate in establishing how they're going to do the Processes. Make them smart in using that power. Organizational engineers orchestrate the organization using the Design and Operation Process while they motivate and empower the people using the Scientific Principles.

Watching/Improving/Changing

We now have a living, breathing organization doing The Task by performing the Processes. It's time to watch how things are going, Step 14. We must now decide what to watch, how to watch it, and set up expectations. If we don't like what we see, or come upon some new vision, we'll change how to do what we're doing or perhaps even change what we're doing. Change is Step 15.

Step 14—Watch

We are now used to the idea that Organizational Engineering is nothing more than the obvious. So, it should be no surprise that what to watch is quite understandable. We watch what we do; each person, each box on the process organization chart, watches their responsibility, their Process, their job. The boss who "owns" The Task box watches how well the organization has been executed. Do all the Processes know what they are suppose to do as defined in steps 6, 7, and 8? And, as mentioned before, are the very important Ground Rules being followed? If so, are these Rules doing their job of keeping the Processes working together properly? The organizational engineer conducts the orchestra of Processes using

The Ground Rules. In the meantime, the Process people watch how well they are doing the Processes. Are they doing them as defined in steps 6, 7, and 8?

A crazy story with a point. Let's say your son or daughter is taking algebra in school. At the end of each chapter in the book, a test is given. But something strange happens. The teacher collects the tests and hands them to the school principal. Neither the teacher nor the students see the results. They just keep on studying, keep on trying to learn new material without knowing if they have learned what they have already studied. The principal sits in the office, grades the tests, and worries about the class because the scores are low. Ridiculous situation? You bet.

What's happening here? The principal is watching what the teacher and students should be watching. The principal gets more upset as test after test shows the students slipping, but the teacher and students just keep moving ahead in the book because they don't know the results. They may be piling mistake on top of mistake. What does this tell us? Those doing the work must be the watchers and improvers of the work, not someone else, not the boss.

This crazy story is not so far fetched. I have seen things just like this actually happen, even in supposedly well-managed companies. People are not watching the right things, and therefore can do nothing about problems because they are not in the position to fix the problems that the watching shows. So what happens? Nothing good. The boss is watching what the Process people should be watching. And, no one is watching what the boss, the organizational engineer, should watch, namely is the organization working per the plan set up by the Organizational Design and Operating Process. (Of course, my observations have been that some organizations don't use any organizing system. Therefore, they have no organizational plan to watch.)

This is a huge problem. People are not watching what they are responsible to do. They are not watching what they do, what they can control. What to watch depends on your role in the organization. The students and teacher should watch and improve their algebra studies, not the principal. Process people should watch how well they are doing their Process that is defined by steps 6, 7 and 8. The organizational engineer should watch his piece of the action: that being the organization itself, the entire plan as laid out by the Organizational Design and Operating Process.

In order to get some results some actions must happen. Actions come before results. Actions are what produce results. Unfortunately, I have seen too often that this is not recognized. Managers start looking for bottom-line results before seeing if the actions are happening as planned. In other words, the first thing to watch should be the actions, namely the organizational plan. This is the job of the organizational engineer. Is the organization functioning like it was planned? Are the Processes happening as defined in the plan? Or, is our operation running in mass confusion, helter-skelter? Don't expect a deck on the back of your house if Fred is building you a doghouse!

Now that we know to watch what we each do, how do we watch? Our standard philosophy applies: we watch as simply as possible. Watching is organizational engineering work; it's one of the steps. Remember, organizational engineering work should be simple, the minimum, yet complete. There are obviously some numbers when it comes to looking at results for our golf ball factory. These numbers may be money (costs, budgets, profits, etc.), golf balls per hour, golf ball machine downtime and repair costs, scrapped golf balls per hour, etc. But, what is the best way to see if our plan of action is being executed, and if it's working right? How does the organizational engineer watch the plan? Yogi Berra is credited with saying something like: "You can observe a lot just by watching." This is an excellent piece of simplicity. And, my experience has convinced me that it works. Just go out and see what's happening, daily.

Organizational engineers should not get trapped into a seriously expensive and destructive trap, a bad habit—MBI. MBI, Management By Isolation, leads to dependence on armies of non-value-added staff people collecting data and making charts to look at in the office, isolating the boss from the Processes doing The Task. The data is not accurate, is misunderstood, and is massaged through the collection and reporting system. Bad decisions come from MBI; Principle 2 is destroyed. The boss is trying to control something at a distance, and is using flawed information for decision-making. This is deadly to an organization. I have seen hundreds of millions of dollars wasted by MBI. Organizational engineers must go out and watch the Processes where they are happening. Are steps 6, 7 and 8 happening and are they working right?

Now that we are watching what we each do, are we happy with what we see? We expect to have repeat business from customers. Are we getting it? If it isn't happening, we've got a problem. Maybe no one likes our golf balls, or our service. Are we making the wrong kind of balls, or are our deliveries always late? Are the golf ball machines broken down too much, say 10% of the time and we expect it should be half that? Are the ball-producing Processes and the maintenance man working well together, or do they need help?

We just slipped into step 15: do something to fix what doesn't meet our expectations. Once we've set up our Watch methods, it's only natural to think about what we see. And, people naturally want to fix a problem that they discover, especially when they have control over what's making the problem and have the authority to do something about it. Or, we may see a new vision of a need or totally new, possibly fantastic opportunity.

Step 15—Fix/Improve/Re-plan

Our final step is not final at all. This step leads back to the others: right back to step one, or maybe step two, or maybe step 8 if the organizational engineer sees a Ground Rule is not working right. Organizations are dynamic; they never become stagnant. They're always on the move, improving or doing something different. Maybe even The Task itself changes.

Again, Principle 2 is the key to this step. The best place to control, fix/improve/re-plan, something is where that something happens. Processes are made better where they happen. The students and the teacher need to be watching their algebra progress and fixing something if the tests, the watching, show help is needed. The golf ball machine operator and his/her boss use the data they collect to see how fast and well the golf balls are produced. If they see a problem or possibility for improvement, they do it. Perhaps someone in sales sees a market, a vision, for a new golf accessory. Meanwhile, organizational engineers watch to see if The Task has been split up into appropriate Processes. Is everything happening that needs to happen? Are the Ground Rules to get the Processes to work together being used and are they getting the job done? The organizational engineer is watching and fixing the organizational plan. The Process people are watching and fixing their Process. Everyone watches their responsibilities then fixes and improves them.

The Whole Ball of Wax
Steps 1 through 15

What is the result of doing the Organizational Design and Operating Process? Your organization and all the people will thrive. Everyone will be doing what he/she is supposed to do. Everyone controls his/her own piece of the action. They are capable because the Scientific Principles see to it. And, motivation to do The

Task is automatic. Your organization is like a whirling mass of water boiling in a pan. And, the boiling starts at the bottom of the organization, where the real work is happening, where The Task is getting done by the Processes. Plus, everyone is doing their part and no one is overloaded; there aren't just a few people hauling the whole load. Organizations set up and operated by people who know and execute The Organizational Engineering Design and Operating Process while using the Scientific Principles are a blast for everyone involved. (Plus, they're profitable.)

Execution—Organizational Engineering in Action

What does it take to be a successful tennis player or football team? There are a lot of good athletes who know their games, know what they should do. The difference between being average and being great is the ability to execute, consistently. Yes, the name of the game is execution: doing what you know you should do, and doing it well. Lots of athletes know their game; the successful ones execute it diligently, consistently.

You have just read a brief description of The Scientific Principles and The Design and Operating Process. Each individual step and Principle can be a lengthy, involved subject. But our goal here has been to set up a system to follow, telling what to do without complicating how each step should be done. Your discretion should be used on the effort required to do each part of the process. A lot depends on the complexity of your vision of a need or possibility, the size of your project. But, each of the fifteen steps must be considered, in sequence, and the Scientific Principles are a must to get people motivated.

By now you must have decided that this whole thing seems way too simple to be successful. For instance, we've only seen dinky little organizations with just two levels. Everyone knows that some projects or organizations are bound to have more than just two levels. Well, you're right. But, for simplicity sake, let's start with that thought.

The Two-Level Concept

Our Process Organization consists of The Task broken down into Processes. That's two levels. Yes, organizations may have more than just two levels. But Organizational Engineering is just a two-level concept. Think simply; think just two levels.

The organizational engineer must execute the Organizational Design and Operating Process and the Scientific Principles to just two levels. The engineer thinks about The Task, steps 1 and 2, of the whole operation, then considers how

The Task is divided into Processes, steps 3, 4, and 5. Steps 6 through 15 supply details of doing The Task and Watching in order to improve or change The Task and/or Processes. All steps are applied to the two levels, using the Scientific Principles all the time. A person responsible for any box on a Process organization chart that has a level of Processes under it is in a Task box; he/she is an organizational engineer, responsible for his/her own "two-level organization."

The Two-Level Concept organization chart (see next page) shows the concept. The Top Task, the very top box on the chart, is the reason for the whole organization to exist. The first five steps divide The (Top) Task into Direct and Support Processes. The organizational engineer, the big boss, executes the rest of the steps for these two levels. This is the first two-level organization established.

Each Process of this first two-level organization may become The Task of a next two-level organization. Notice how Make Golf Balls becomes The Task of the next two-level organization. The people involved in those two levels now execute Organizational Engineering to those two levels, starting with their Task. So, a Process from the top two-level organization becomes The Task of the next two levels. Et cetera, Et cetera, Et cetera.

The Two-Level Concept

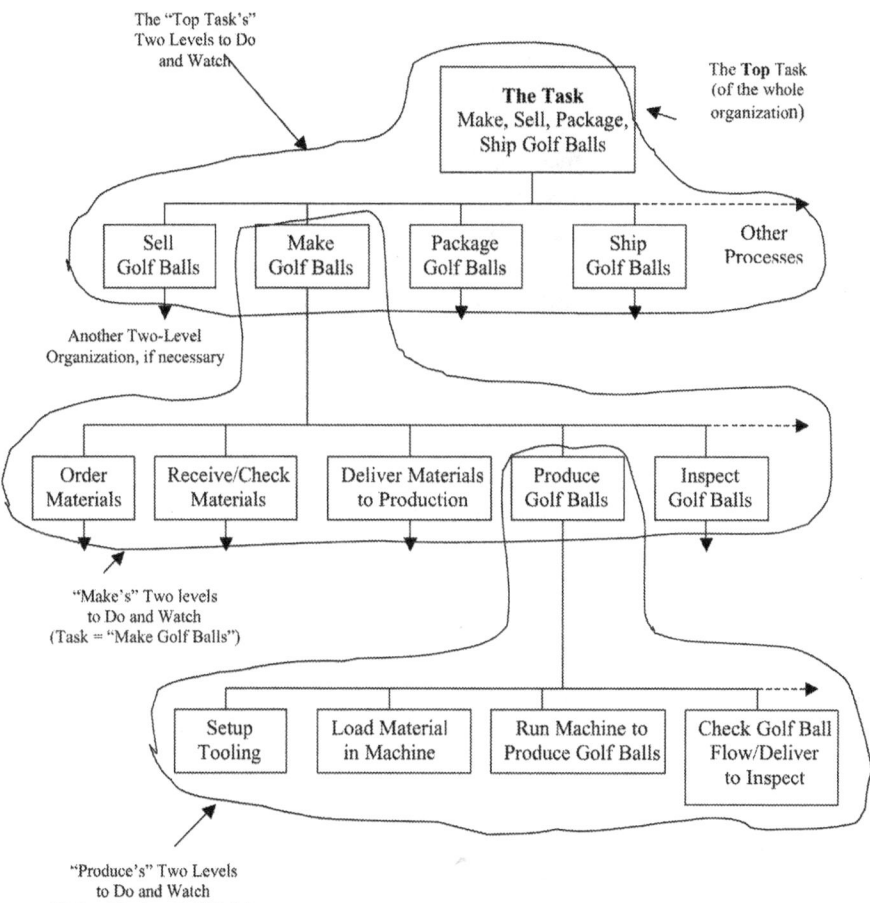

The "Top Task's"
Two Levels to Do
and Watch

The **Top** Task
(of the whole
organization)

The Task
Make, Sell, Package,
Ship Golf Balls

Sell
Golf Balls

Make
Golf Balls

Package
Golf Balls

Ship
Golf Balls

Other
Processes

Another Two-Level
Organization, if necessary

Order
Materials

Receive/Check
Materials

Deliver Materials
to Production

Produce
Golf Balls

Inspect
Golf Balls

"Make's" Two levels
to Do and Watch
(Task = "Make Golf Balls")

Setup
Tooling

Load Material
in Machine

Run Machine to
Produce Golf Balls

Check Golf Ball
Flow/Deliver
to Inspect

"Produce's" Two Levels
to Do and Watch
(Task = "Produce Golf Balls")

"The Task" of any two levels is any box
that has a level below it.

Whoa, another row of boxes, and another? What happened to simplicity? What happened to "minimizing organizational engineering work?" This is where your thinking is required. Remember the Scientific Principles will unleash people's brains, energy, and motivation. Do not, do not keep breaking down each Process into more Tasks; do not build a zillion level Process Organization. Yes, this is a judgment call; hopefully it is based on your new knowledge of the concept of Organizational Engineering. Fortunately, there is help here. Should your chart go too far your motivated people, doing the processes, will let you know.

Maybe this will help? Tasks, boxes on the org chart, are "what to do". Somewhere your organization chart will end. What ends it is step 7: Process methods. Step 7 is how you're going to do what the Process box says. Stop building the org chart and define how the bottom Process box is to be done. For instance, "Run Machine to Produce Golf Balls" could be broken down to another level of more sub-Tasks. But, this is not necessary if you properly write step 7 process methods for "Run Machine..."

Perhaps you already noticed that people in the middle levels are very key players. That is because they are actually involved in three levels, all the time. They're involved in two two-level organizations. For instance, look at the position of Make The Golf Balls.

That box is a Direct Process of the top two-level organization; it then becomes The Task of the next two-level organization. So, the organizational engineer in that position plays a role in both of these two-level organizations. The guy in the middle always gets squeezed; he/she is a Process and a Task at the same time. He/she must understand the role and watch their particular Process, then convert it to a Task that is then broken down into its own Processes. First he/she is a subordinate, receiving a Process from their Task boss. Second, he/she is the organizational engineer of his/her own Task and executes Organizational Engineering to that two-level organization.

Through all of this the Scientific Principles become very important. As The Processes pass on down to the final, bottom level every person is shown the whole scheme and how their efforts help achieve the Top Task. This is Principle 3: tell people everything.

The Multi-Level Concept

Okay, I lied. There is more than the Two-Level Concept. But, it takes priority. If every organizational engineer of each two-levels does not execute all of Organizational Engineering, The Scientific Principles and The Design and Operating Process, the whole organization will suffer. But, there's more. The people in the upper levels of your Process Organization also watch all the way down. The multi-level concept says that people in boxes that have multiple levels below must observe how things are going all the way down. For example, the Top Task boss of our golf ball company should see how Order Materials, or Produce Golf Balls is doing. That's two levels below his/her box.

But we just emphasized the two-level concept. How does this fit together? Two benefits result from the top boss going out to see how Order Materials is doing, or for that matter Load Material in Machine, even another level down. First, it shows the people in those Processes that the big boss, levels up from their piece of the action, is truly interested. People are people; motivation is motivation. Second, the big boss is doing nothing more than his/her part of Watching/Improving/Changing, steps 14 and 15. The big boss is seeing if his/her organizational engineers of the Tasks below are doing their job. That is, are they executing organizational engineering, all of it?

Yes, the boss is involved in multi-levels. Has the big boss taught Organizational Engineering to the Task bosses below? Have those organizational engineers defined each of the boxes below them and set up the Ground Rules in that level so that their Task is done according to the plan? Are they using the Scientific Principles by telling people everything and getting them involved in developing methods to do the Processes? And on, and on, and on.

However, the big boss must not go out on the floor and start giving instructions or start changing everyone's Ground Rules on the other two-level organizations below. When out on the production floor, the big boss is merely watching and analyzing. Should questions arise, the boss talks with his/her subordinate organizational engineers. The big boss executes step 15 (Fix/Improve/Re-plan) on the top two levels. Horribly confusing messes are made when bosses start directly horning in on things happening multiple levels below. People get confused; they don't trust their direct boss, their organizational engineer. Both The Task and the people suffer. If there are problems levels below, the big boss has not properly empowered the organizational engineers in those two-level organizations; he/she has not executed Organizational Engineering properly.

What Happens At The Bottom?

So, each organizational engineer handles his/her two-level organization. What about the folks doing the Processes on the bottom of the chart, those who actually do the productive work? Knowing that The Task is all-important, we recognize that these folks are actually the most important of all. They are doing what the whole organization was established to do.

These people at the bottom also have two levels to watch, plus more. First they must understand their Task and Processes and be directly involved in the steps to set up efficient methods and interactions at their level. They help their boss execute Organizational Engineering to their bottom two-level organization. In order to do that they need to know how their two levels fit in with those farther up and those to the side on the Process Organization chart. Remember, Process Organizations are not built of individually isolated pieces. A Process Organization is one cohesive effort composed of all the pieces needed to get The Task, The Top Task done. And, it is no more than that. There should be no irrelevant, superfluous processes, people, or activities.

The boiling, whirling activity of change, improvement, and energy is most vigorous at the bottom. That is as it should be. The maximum effort is at the productive level, the value-added level. Minimum efforts are the Organizational Engineering work.

So, you organizational engineers be ready. All those people doing the productive work will have more ideas, more energy than you can imagine. The Scientific Principles have unleashed that power of the sun. Change will be a part of daily life.

The Process Organization in Action

Your organization is unique. You may be taking on a Task similar to someone else's; that's what competition is all about. But, there are an infinite number of ways to get something done.

Let's take a quick look at a sample, a portion of a simplified golf ball manufacturer. It is another look at a Task being divided into Processes, each becoming Tasks of the next two-level organization, etc. down the chart. The Direct Processes for each Task are connected with solid lines while Support Processes are connected by dotted lines.

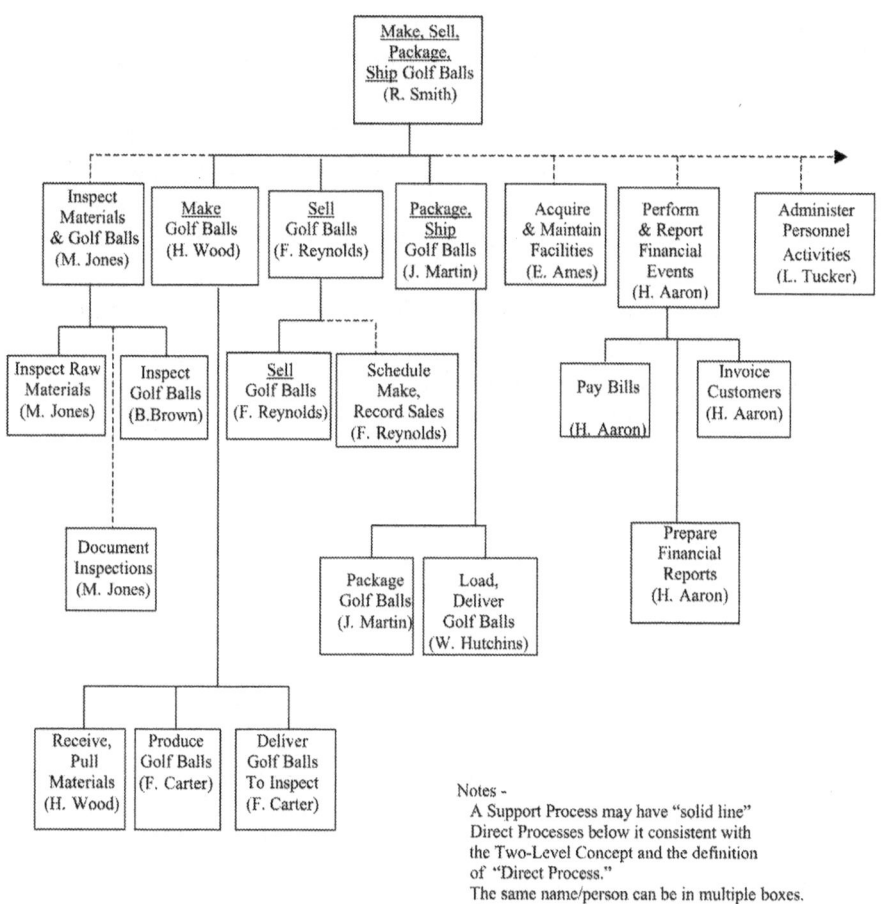

Notes -
   A Support Process may have "solid line"
   Direct Processes below it consistent with
   the Two-Level Concept and the definition
   of "Direct Process."
   The same name/person can be in multiple boxes.
   A person may perform more than one process.

Sample of a Process Organization

There are some important things to notice. First, there are Direct Processes, like Pay Bills, under a Task that was originally a Support Process, Perform/Report Financial Events. Why? Think two-level organizations. Pay Bills is a Direct Process of Perform/Report Financial Transactions. The organizational engineer responsible for that Task sees Pay Bills as a Direct Process. Second, look at the names. The same name may appear in more than one box; the same person may have more than one responsibility in the organization. Why? Think Process Organization, not "people organization." Process Organizations get The Task done. People organizations get confused. The Process Organization Chart shows what needs to happen, what the organization does. People organization charts show people's names and titles, Big Deal! Remember the reason for the chart is to show what the organization does, not just show people's names. Also, there are no (people) titles shown in the chart. But, now that you know what must happen, and have Tasks assigned to people, go ahead and give people titles if you wish. You can even use that word "manager," if you want.

"Half-Baked" or "Burnt to a Crisp"! How far goes our Process Organization Chart? How many levels, how many two-level organizations, should the chart have? Go too far, the organization will be burnt to a crisp. Don't go far enough, it's half-baked.

Remember, your Process Organization is unique. It is built to suit The Task and what it takes to do that Task. How far the chart breaks The Task down, how many two-level organizations it has, is a judgment call. Experience says keep your Process Organization Chart "high-level," as flat as possible, containing as few levels as possible. Each box on the organization chart represents either The Task or The Processes: steps 2, 3 and 4. As mentioned before, Step 7 ends additional layers on the chart by describing all it takes to do what is in that box. There will be no need for additional levels when the productive work actually gets accomplished by doing the step 7 methods. The org chart is done. No more levels.

Let's say you want a deck on the back of you house. Whether you know it or not, you do the Design and Operating Process, probably in your head. You decide that you need a deck (step 1) and how big it should be and how it should look (step 2). Then you go through, perhaps only mentally without writing anything down, the rest of the steps in order. What you've really done is build a two-level Process Organization. The Task is from step 2: how big it should be and what it should look like. The Processes are things like: Design The Deck, Obtain Materials, Obtain Tools Needed, Build The Deck, Paint The Deck, etc. Your step 7 methods for each of these Processes will finish your planning of what to do and how to do it. Your Org Chart is finished. (Of course, your planning is not fully complete until you schedule the project and get materials.) You need no more levels, no more boxes. It's a simple Task that's not too big, not too spread out geographically, etc.

Now let's say you decide to build and sell automobiles, lots of automobiles. The same thing happens. You gaze into the crystal ball and visualize selling a million cars a year, a car of new design. You decide the market is ready for a sports car that looks like a Bradley tank. Obviously, this is a bigger Task than building a deck on the back of your house. Interestingly enough your first two levels may look exactly like those for building the deck. The Task is similar: Design and Build sport cars that look like miniature Bradley tanks. The Processes may be almost the same: Design The Car, Obtain Materials, Obtain Tools, Build the Cars, etc., plus some support Processes. But, in this case Obtain Tools may have many more considerations than tools required to build the deck. You'll need land, buildings, and machinery. You may have multiple levels below "Obtain Tools".

So, how far you go in "leveling" your organization is a judgment call. Think. There is help here, though. Organizational Engineering will help later if you have incorrectly "leveled" your organization. Steps 14 and 15 provide the tools to watch and fix your organization if it is not working well. Personally, I would go half-baked at first, not establishing enough levels and pushing the bottom Process boxes to do a lot in their methods, step 7. Flatten the organization; minimize Organizational Engineering while maximizing productive work. Minimum organizations work a whole lot better that confusing, monstrous organizations.

Lessons Learned

This description of Organizational Engineering is brief. Some people might say too brief. Well, it's brief because getting organized is a simple concept. "It is simple to make something complex, but complex to make something simple." This concept is the culmination of decades of study, experience and experiment with management philosophies, concepts, and theories. It has been a complex journey to simplicity. **Do not make Organizational Engineering complicated.**

We have been brief because I have a great deal of respect for the normal person's intellect, ability to think, and innate interest in doing the right things right. They don't need volumes of words; all they need is this simple method and their brain. Think and execute the Organizational Design and Operating Process while applying the Scientific Principles. Don't rush it. Don't skip steps.

Someone once asked me what I thought to be the worst single trait of a poorly run organization. There are tons of details involved, but in my experience the thing that has struck me the most is the destruction of Scientific Principle 2: the best place to control something is where that something takes place. By the way, are those the exact words? I'm into the concept, not memorizing exact wording.

Why should this strike me so? Probably because it can destroy the rest of the Principles; and the Principles are important, almost more important than the Design and Operating Process. If you decide to manage an organization by trying to directly control all of its pieces, you have destroyed the organization, the people, and The Task. If you could do all of everything instantaneously everywhere in the organization, you wouldn't need the organization; it's a one-man show. There's nothing wrong with that, I guess. I suppose you can set up and operate a one-man latte stand and do everything required. But, as soon as you start needing other people to do things while you do something else, like execute Organizational Engineering, you have to let go. You must empower them by using the Scientific Principles.

Some pages back we visited a situation in which a personnel department was allowed to snuff out some good ideas on a production floor. People twenty miles away from the plant were allowed to stop an improvement that all the productive people had developed. The suits "controlled" the operation; or better, they "uncontrolled" it. Ignorance prevailed. The organization suffered, terribly. Remember MBI (Management by Isolation); it's devastating.

On the other hand, I had the chance to see a most intense application of Principle 2, and for that matter the other Principles. I had the very good fortune of operating a department in a heavy industrial plant, reporting to the General Manager of the plant. He was the finest example of a master of Organizational Engineering I have ever personally observed. I don't think he knew he was an organizational engineer as described here, but he was doing it. The plant was saddled with a rather serious, expensive problem. Our department had full responsibility for the subject; it was part of our department's Task. A somewhat unusual solution to this problem was developed. Unfortunately, there was an element of risk involved, a very large element. While the General Manager, who wasn't twenty miles away but right on the scene, was concerned and open for discussion, he made it eminently clear that control of our Task was up to us, the department. To be quite honest I was a bit surprised. The risk was so great I would have almost felt relieved if he had over-ridden our choice to take it. But, he didn't—major lesson in control where it should be. Get the right people in the right place, empower them, etc. (By the way, we were lucky. The solution worked.)

So, use the Principles. Execute Organizational Engineering. You'll have the right people in the right place, doing and improving.

Now comes a favorite subject of mine—Complainers. If there is anything that an organization needs the most it is people with energy, people with the power of the sun. Unfortunately, there seem to be very few organizations that execute Organizational Engineering. Some do some of it; some do none of it. Complainers are ignored. What a loss to the organization.

Organizations should have complainers. They are energetic. They have ideas. They express ideas. They are a golden thorn in management's side. The trick is in how the organization handles the complainers. Sometimes they are shuffled from group to group. Sometimes they are snuffed out, fired or shoved in the corner. They either end up leaving or they shut up, sit in the corner, and collect a paycheck. The organization loses something precious. But, thank goodness in some places they are mined. Yes, complainers are like a vein of gold. The Scientific Principles are the pick and shovel.

Mining complainers is a win-win situation. There is no losing. You get one of two things. If that thorn in your side has some really good ideas, you've struck pay dirt. If that thorn in your side just doesn't understand some things, you'll get an informed, energetic participant. Remember, Never Say No communication? It works; it's Principle 3. You can't lose, but it takes work. Do it. Communicate.

We now tackle a controversial subject that I haven't spent much time on: money. Many high-powered leaders could really beat me up over that. If they've read this far they probably already would like to take me on. We've been saying: "forget the money." Remember making money is not The Task. If all everyone understood The Task is "to make money", we'd have no food, cars, water, houses, etc.

Remember, I have an ally in this regard, someone I mentioned a few pages back. As the keynote speaker at a graduation ceremony his message was: "Don't do it for the money." Do something worthwhile and do it well. The money will come. Money is a by-product of being productive.

That's not to say money is not important. It's obvious that it is. But, there is a less than obvious reason that it is important; it has to do with Organizational Engineering. Money is one of the best instruments used to do step 14, Watch. Yes, money is a great watching device. It tells you a lot. Did you pick the right thing to do? In other words, will people buy what you decided to do; is it worthwhile? Are you doing it well? Is Make The Golf Balls operating within its budget so that your planned bottom line, your profit comes out as planned? Yes, you must watch the money, but it is not The Task. If you disagree, think ENRON—people pulling financial hocus pocus but not doing the real Task of their organization.

While we're on the subject of money there is a rather interesting phenomena to discuss which directly affects your organization's financial interests: the costs of MBI in action. Those costs are both financial and emotional.

I worked for a large outfit that is the very epitome of MBI. And, it does not seem to know or understand its predicament. You can't run a private, "profit-making" enterprise any worse, but it does still struggle along. (Why it's still in existence is another story.) Operating under the MBI concept, the information required for the management to control the organization from afar must be provided through a network of organizational levels and armies of staff people involved in non-value added work. This outfit has hundreds of watching methods: thousands of charts and graphs of nitty-gritty data. As it turns out not all the charts are exactly accurate, for political reasons. And, not all pertinent data is presented on the charts. But, the big rub here is this: the reasons behind the numbers on the charts are not understood. The charts don't really say what's going on out where The Task is being performed. MBI (isolation and ignorance) prevails.

So what? Decisions to control operations are made by people who are isolated from where the data comes, and they are dealing with much massaged data. Misinterpretation of the real story is standard operation. This costs in two ways, financial and emotional, which leads to more financial costs. First, the overhead staff to produce the zillions of inaccurate charts is an absolute army costing millions. And, the decisions miss the mark. Total new plants have been erected to expand capabilities already in existence, operations that are running poorly. Instead of fixing the existing capability, entire new operations are added. Hundreds of millions, no billions of dollars right down the drain. And, both the existing and the new plants are run using the same "management" method. Second, while the people in the trenches are somewhat entertained by the comedy they are observing, this is a very frustrating situation for those people doing the productive work, or better, trying to do the productive work. They would like to help, but that's not in the cards. Those who think they are in control are out of reach. Attitudes plummet. This organization has lost its people, its power of the sun—a costly blow.

Jacobson's Law: "The less work an organization produces, the more frequently it reorganizes." I had this in a pile of notes. I have found Jacobson's Law to be alive and thriving.

I don't know who Jacobson is or was, but I have observed an organization that epitomizes his Law. There is a continual reorganization effort in progress. No, this is not just normal adjustments needed in a changing organization; these are major upheavals cutting right to the core of distributing The Task into Processes. This constant change is required because they never seem to achieve an effective, efficient organization. The re-org is executed by some mysterious philosophy, nothing like Organizational Engineering. However, there is a common thread to all the re-org efforts: they are simple for the management to execute, because the management people don't have to do much. "It is simple to make something complex."

There are many other lessons learned. But, I've said enough. So, take a shot at Organizational Engineering: The Organizational Design and Operating Process using The Scientific Principles. Make the "complex" simple. Execute. Minimize Org Engineering work. Maximize productive work. Keep your Process Organization as simple, the org chart as flat, as possible. Apply the Scientific Principles; people are the key.

You organizational engineers—rip out the next page and hang it on the wall. It's one page to a thriving and fun organization.

Paul

The Scientific Principles

#1—To successfully get something done that requires a group to do, the whole group must want to get the same thing done.

#2—The best place to control something is where that something takes place.

#3—The more information people are given about things that affect getting results, the more they will work to reach those results.

#4—People given the chance to help decide how to get something done will then want to get it done.

The Organizational Design and Operating Process

What To Do
 1. Envision A Need Or Possibility
 2. Understand The Task
 3. Identify Direct Processes To Do The Task
 4. Identify Support Processes
 5. Make A Process Organization Chart
 6. Define And Set The Boundaries Of The Processes
 7. Establish Process Methods
 8. Develop Ground Rules For The Chart
 9. Establish Rules For Everyone
 10. Sequence & Schedule The Action
 11. Identify What's Needed To Do This
Doing It
 12. Find People
 13. Empower The People
Watching/Improving/Changing
 14. Watch
 15. Fix/Improve/Re-plan

0-595-30676-4